# PRAISE FOR

MW01229103

*Finding Home* is my favorite kind of story. It's true, full of surprises, and deliciously sprinkled with wit and humor. Rod's trust in Christ shines forth beautifully in this book, sparking hope.

Melinda Spears Rogers
Minister to Children
Christ Chapel Bible Church

———

What would you give to be walking on air? In *Finding Home*, Rod Butler lives and shares this experience with his own unique wit and humor. This book is a steady beam of joy in an increasingly dark and dreary world.

Daniel Miller
Graphic Designer

———

This is Rod's story, with all the ups and downs, spiced with his great sense of humor, seasoned with poetry quips at the end of each chapter. I absolutely love this book!

Debi Barton
Wife, Mother, Grandmother, and Poet Wannabe

What a great journey! I enjoyed reading about Rod's child-hood and how music factored into so many areas of his life. His explanation of a life with Jesus is clear and compelling, and his love for the Lord shines through the words he's written. And, throughout this book I was laughing out loud.

Staci Mauney

Prestige Prose

———

Understanding, acceptance, and transformed life...Rod shares his humorous, encouraging story in a way that helps us understand God's all-transforming love.

Karen Wimberley

Wife, Mother, Grandmother

———

*Finding Home* is a journey that rolls through all the twists and turns of life. Along the way, Jesus Christ launches new life and new hope. A delightful read. I highly recommend it.

Rebecca Peterson

Children's Pastor, Retired

This book is filled with humor, "Aha!" moments, and profound truths. Rod's life-path reveals the unexpected ways we learn and grow. It's a great read for teens, moms, dads—and grannies!

Nancy Kort
Retired Federal Executive

———

Rod Butler writes like he talks, which makes his writing so appealing! You will enjoy *Finding Home*, watching how God uses our experiences to point people to the Light.

Sandy Golden
Former KCBI Radio Personality
(and Mom to a Grade-schooler
Who Loved Listening to KZ Rod)

# FINDING HOME

## MY FUNNY JOURNEY INTO FAITH

ROD BUTLER

Filament City
Media

*For Bessie Galloway, long deceased, yet I still hear your voice:*
*"Give them the literature."*

"They desire a better country, that is, a heavenly one."
Hebrews 11:16

# CONTENTS

# FOREWORD

Have you ever been homesick?

Maybe it was your first-ever night at camp. The people were all strangers. The food was mystery meat and pickled beets. It was so hard to climb up on your bunk and now you were afraid of falling off. And if you did fall off, you were worried about what would be down there—bats and snakes and spiders! So you spent the whole night curled up in a tight ball at the bottom of your bedroll, in anguished longing for your bed with its Mickey Mouse sheets and the sound of your dad laughing at late-night TV from the family room.

Or maybe it was your first trip back home after a semester away at college. You had been loving campus life, your new friends, the professors, and even cafeteria food, but suddenly, Dad's ridiculous puns, Mom's pecan pie and endless questions, and even the puppy-scented hugs from your sticky baby brother seem so urgently desired that you're willing to pay the fine for speeding, just to fling open the door and be at home five minutes sooner.

As Rod leads you through his stories of childhood with candor and humor, I think you may find, like I did, that his experiences resonate with many of your own, and the folks that peopled his growing up years will take on such colorful personas that you will think of them as common friends.

But this is the story of another kind of home, as well, and as Rod shares, in words as true and sweet and simple as the breakfast your grandma cooked for you after a sleepover, you may find yourself developing that same deep longing for that place too. A distant place, yet a familiar place. As warm and close as sweet fellowship in the church meeting hall, yet a place with untouched grandeur that waits beyond our imagination.

All of this reminds me of a story about a horse named Paint.

If you've ever rented a horse to ride from a commercial stable, then you probably know what happens when you reach the farthest end of the trail. On the way out, good ole Paint is the model mount, responding instantly to your lightest touch of the reigns, and you can play out all sorts of fantasies involving yourself dashing into danger on your mighty steed to save the day.

But the very second that you turn back toward the stable, good ole Paint becomes a single-minded, uncontrollable machine, and all you can do is grip the saddle horn and hang on as the horse gallops in a straight line, on the trail or not, never wavering, never slowing down, until he reaches the stable, where he knows the saddle will come off and water and oats are waiting.

It is possible that by the end of this book that you, like me, will be like that horse, racing with a glad determination that can't be held back, toward what your heart has always longed for: home!

Martha Singleton
Author
*Multiple Choice, The View through Your Window, Let It Shine*

# FUNNY YOU SHOULD ASK

Can faith be funny? Do those two words, faith and funny, belong together?

I mean, most church services are serious.

Most sermons provide instruction, with maybe a cute or clever story thrown in.

When you open a religious book, you'll usually find theology, applied theology, and Bible commentary, and if certain parts are lighthearted, they're usually brief.

Practical Christian living books are plentiful, stocking shelves, but probably they're not funny. Maybe a smile here and there, an anecdote, a side comment, but not a lot of funny business salt and peppered through the pages.

That's what we expect, right?

Then along comes this Butler guy with a book called *Finding Home*. That seems to carry a spiritual undertone. But then, the subtitle:

*My Funny Journey into Faith.* Funny journey?

Can there be a "funny" journey into faith?

I'm glad you asked. Or, hopefully...you're glad I asked.

And here's my answer: Yes. The faith journey can be amusing, delightful, even ha-ha hilarious, interwoven through the major threads of inspiration, contemplation, and revelation.

But there's a higher source that proves that funny fits into faith. The highest source.

The Bible, our most amazing book, God's Book, wraps together history, theology, poetry, wisdom, suspense, frights and sights, and yes, many instances of funny, woven tightly into the narrative.

Perhaps the word "funny" is misleading. Perhaps God's Word is seasoned with delight, laughter, exaggeration, surprise, reversal, humorous dialogue, and almost comical situations.

For example...

Consider this wonderful statement: Abraham went out, not knowing where he was going. That's funny, in a profound sort of way.

Jesus put forth parables that were startling, engaging to the point of funniness. Think of the camel going through the eye of a needle or faith as small as a mustard seed moving a mountain. Or a man with a log in his eye, attempting to remove from another man's eye a tiny speck.

God gave a donkey the ability to speak. The animal famous for braying out, "Heee-haww!"

Abraham's wife Sarah, in her nineties, having a baby, and the baby's name? Isaac, which means "he laughs."

What about Gideon dreaming of a bread roll that tumbled down a hill and flattened an enemy's tent?

Or Ecclesiastes reminding us that there's a time to weep *and* a time to laugh.

And Proverbs 17:22 making a deep, lasting impression about the healing power of humor, saying "A merry heart does good, like medicine."

So it's true.

Scripture includes humor, alongside all the other facets of life.

And this book includes humor. Often side-by-side with sincere faith.

I guess the only way I know how to tell any story is with humor included. And that's okay, isn't it? Because:

A merry heart is something we all need. And I don't really know how to *not* be funny.

I blame my father mainly. He was a professional scriptwriter and a humorist by nature. I only knew him a few years, but—very sneakily—he made sure I had enough giggle-blood in my veins to laugh—I mean last—a lifetime.

My mother was funny without meaning to be. My grandmother too. Their reason was learning English as a third or fourth language and sometimes confusing words without knowing it.

And my brother, Mark, and his wife, Bonnie? Professional comedians without the professional part. And across the years, God has placed into my life so many individuals who are encouraging, wise, talented, and flat-out funny.

So you see, I was surrounded. There wasn't any way to stop the funny.

And as a Christian storyteller, I've come to cherish the stories that bring both a smile and a message. I've loved following creatives like C.S. Lewis, G.K. Chesterton, Michelangelo, and J.S. Bach—all of them, and many others, blending delight and devotion.

I hope that this book will combine elements in that same way and, most importantly, be a bright, beautiful blessing, specifically, for you.

Let our funny journey begin.

Rod Butler
Granbury, Texas
September 19, 2022

# PART ONE
## Before

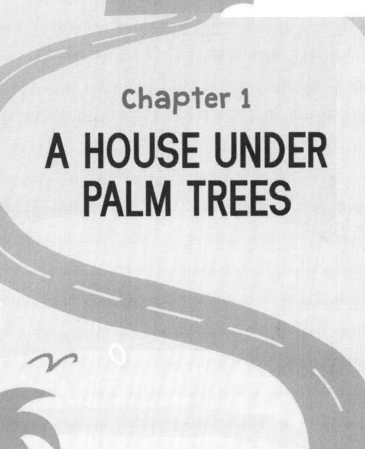

# Chapter 1
# A HOUSE UNDER PALM TREES

I KNOW I WAS BORN BECAUSE WE GOT A RECEIPT. YOU KNOW, A birth certificate.

I still have it. (Always save your receipts.) The certificate, old but official, certifies that on December 19, 1955, at 6:09 a.m., in Los Angeles County, at the Santa Monica Hospital, located in, um, Santa Monica, on a Monday, Roderick Paul Butler was born.

Monday. I've always liked Monday, my first day on the planet.

The registration district number was 7080, registrar's number 53210. Date received by local registrar was December 23, 1955 (hmm, guess they mailed it), and the attendant was John F. Duge, MD. Good work, Dr. Duge, and thank you.

At the time, my mother was thirty-four years old, my dad forty-four. The residence listed on the birth certificate was my parents' second house, located on beautiful Valley Vista Boulevard, Sherman Oaks, California. A curving, sloping, magical street it was, lined by palm trees, breathing under clear blue skies. And graced by a special kind of light, emanating a soft, cheery brightness found only in Southern Cali. I loved walking that street, down to Ventura Boulevard, home of Neff's Toys, and later, the La Reina theater and a record store called the Hippodrome. Wow, dude. Very sixties.

I know my dad lived in that little house with my mom (I've got a few pictures), but when my memories begin, they were divorced, and he had already moved out and was living in an apartment in Studio City. I was driven to that two-bedroom apartment every other Sunday afternoon, and when the door opened, there he was, John Keith Butler. Round face, receding hair line, a bit heavy, big smile, large as life. "Come on in, Rod-Pal." On in I went.

I'd sit on the sofa, watching TV, while he finished writing a script on his typewriter, keys furiously snapping. From that imagination machine came stories for Dime Detective, often featuring his tough, cab-driving hero, Steve Midnight.

After he wrote for the pulp magazines, he switched to movie writing, pumping out tons of scripts for Republic Studios, where John Wayne got his start and Roy Rogers filmed several motion pictures. You can find the name John K. Butler in the credits on *My Pal Trigger*, *Silver Spurs*, and a long list of others.

He was a real-life cowboy too—or at least he dressed like one. And he had a horse, Prince, upon whom I would ride, as Dad led us slowly along the tree-lined trails of Griffith Park. Prince was older and, at one point, threw off his rider—my dad—who landed on his back, which may have been what later triggered an aneurysm that ended his life so abruptly.

He was also an alcoholic, which may have contributed to my parents' divorce. Or it may have been that she was a nonstop talker, and he needed quiet-private to write. He did fight his addiction, joining Alcoholics Anonymous and helping others who were mastered by the drink. I remember an article in their monthly magazine, "Christmas Illumination," in which he described driving by the Valley Vista house, recently divorced, and (against his better judgment), stopping and parking, trying to see what was happening in the living room. There was Roddy, his little boy, alone by the Christmas tree. Dad loved decorating the tree, and it must have been like a thud-to-the-heart from Steve Midnight's billy club, pounding in the impact of his aloneness.

My house under the palm trees was very special, with a double backyard, one part a mowed lawn and rock-floored patio, then through tall hedging and into the second part: a more unkept mini-forest with a tilted storage shed that later became my Time Tunnel laboratory. And the location for one of several homemade monster movies created by my best friend, Kirk Roderick, and yours truly.

From the street, the house was typical of any you'd find in the San Fernando Valley. Painted a light blue, with board and baton siding, a vine-covered front porch, window-paned front door, and by that door, a humble bush, offering the royal sweetness of gardenias, my mother's favorite flower. A small front yard, off the garage, was edged by a wooden white-picket fence and guarded valiantly by the towering palms, which always reminded me of a tree-like version of the Beatles.

My room was very special. Not as fantastic as Disneyland in Anaheim, but close.

I stocked the shelves with spaceships, monster models, science fiction paperback books (Bradbury, Asimov, Heinlein), and collectible bobblehead figures from popular TV shows (Munsters, Addams Family). On a chest with a fold-down desk stood a tall lamp. Funny old thing. It was made from a real trumpet. A trumpet with a lampshade over it. Probably came from Dad.

I didn't have a brother or a sister. Well, not completely true—more to come on that. But for about two weeks, I had a puppy. I named him Ringo, after the Beatles' drummer, of course. Like other puppies in Ringo's family, he didn't live very long, but the special love between a kid and his dog made a deep impression on me. To this day, sorry to say, we've never had a dog. But I'm a dog's best friend, usually bonding with every pooch I meet.

Before moving on, you need to meet my mother, Marguerite Koppl Butler.

Picture a slender, no, a skinny lady with blonde hair and what might sound like a German accent, but she was actually from Czechoslovakia. She was a chatterbox, but a clever one, often funny and very intelligent. Maggie, as friends called her, learned English long after she learned Czech, German, and French.

Amazingly, once her family immigrated to the United States, rushing out of their homeland as Hitler's forces swept in, they quickly adjusted to American life, and Maggie picked up a job in Southern California as a script-proofer. I'm pretty sure that was how she met my dad.

They married June 14, 1948, and though their marriage was not long-lived, thankfully I arrived (I have the certificate), and we were a three-person family for a few years. She and John sailed on his sailboat, Whisper, out of San Pedro, and both rode horses in Griffith Park, Dad riding Toby, Mom riding Tarzan. I imagine those were good days, even though, much too soon, those days unraveled and fell apart.

After that, it was me and my mom at Denny's or Kerry's Coffee Shop on Ventura, eating dinner. I ate my macaroni and cheese; she talked and talked and talked, while her salad got warm and her coffee grew cold.

If we ate at home, we had two options: Swanson's TV dinners or Stouffer's TV dinners. She didn't cook. Well, she made one dish that she took to parties now and then: a plate of asparagus. For a skinny person, she was strangely fearful of gaining weight. She ate dietetic cookies, drank coffee, and nibbled on cold cheeseburgers brought back from Carl's Jr. The Carl's Famous Star with cheese, if you must know.

I was kind of embarrassed when kids would come over. They'd want to open the fridge to see what we had, and it was always disappointing. Or like a visit to the Twilight Zone.

Inside, usually: a boxed chocolate pie from Marie Callender's (plastic fork in crust), the aforementioned sleeping cheeseburger with a bag of frigid fries, and most memorably, an unforgettable water bottle.

Roundish it was, made of glass tinted a pale green, with an eerie resemblance to a stomach as it narrowed up to a spout, like an esophagus, with a cap on top. When half-filled with water (tinted a pale green), that alone made someone want to close the door. And call their mom for pickup.

Really, I had a good life with my mom. Granted, it was unique and not *Leave it to Beaver*, as they say, but it was memorable. And in her way, she loved me. She made me laugh and touched my heart.

Laughter came from just being who she was.

Walking around the house, singing, in that accent, "Oh my dah-ling, oh my dah-ling, oh my dah-ling Clementine!" Which was not really sung but sing-spoken in an off-key voice.

Playing her records: Danny Kaye singing the LA Dodgers theme song or music by The Kingston Trio, the Brothers Four, or the Limeliters.

Saying funny things that were not intended to be funny but were very funny due to English being a later language.

When, at the Sizzler, the waiter asked her if she wanted the all-you-can-eat buffet, and she answered, "No. That's *more* than I can eat."

When, later in life, she met the pastor of the church where I was employed, Pastor Randolph, and proudly announced, "I love this church! I can arrive late and leave early!"

And after getting a part-time job at the church's day care, which was not a good fit for her, she grew tired of a toddler tossing a rattle out of the crib and forcefully proclaimed, "If I ever have another baby, it won't be *you!*"

My favorite heart-touching moment arrived every Valentine's Day. She handed me an oversized—well, to me, gigantic—card, the same one each year, signed with that year's date and printed on the front: "Honey, I looked all over town for a Valentine's card that would show how much I love you." Then, on the inside, "But they didn't have one big enough."

*A house on a street, memories with smiles,*
*Small simple steps, before they became miles.*

# Chapter 2
# MUTTI AND ME

Two words.

Wiener schnitzel.

Or as I pronounced it, "Veener schnitchel."

Dictionaries define it as:

—a breaded veal cutlet, variously seasoned or garnished

—a large thin escalope of veal, coated in egg and crumbs, fried, and traditionally served with a garnish.

[1860–65; < German, = *Weiner* Viennese + *Schnitzel* cutlet, chop]

I mention weiner schnitzel in connection with my grandmother, Maria Koppl, or Mutti, for three reasons:

3. It was the best meal of my entire childhood.

2. It was made with her magical European touch.

1. It somehow *was* Mutti, represented in food form: unique, charming, thoughtful, loving, kind and...unforgettable.

A few Mutti memories:

**Her name.** I called her Mutti. This is a shortened version of the traditional German word for mother: mutter. Interesting that it wasn't the word for grandmother, it was a generation closer, and all three grandkids called her Mutti. Such a sweet name.

**Her food.** The schnitzel was served with carrot slices and new potatoes, which she described as "suft but not too suft." Also, a glass of Hawaiian Punch, with a clear plastic stir-stick that had a small whistle at the end. And what she called "ordervers," Ritz crackers with ham and cheese, peanut butter and jelly, or sour cream and jelly.

**Her phrases.** Instead of "We'll cross that bridge when we come to it," Mutti said: "Dear, ve cross zat bridge until it comes to it." When looking at pictures of our first child, her first great-grand-child, she said: "Zeese pictures...one is more beautiful than ze next." In Mutti-talk, "Thanks, dear" sounded like "Sanks, deah."

**Our walks into the hills.** Back in the 1930s, living in Europe, Mutti and her husband Rudolph would hike cross-country, skiing down amazing, white-blanketed slopes. No wonder, when she and I would walk the rolling sidewalks of Sherman Oaks, I would struggle to keep up with the rhythmic strides of her legs. We would often kick a stone as we walked...from her kick, the stone shot forward, perfectly. From my kick—well, never mind.

**Her voice on the telephone.** When Mutti connected with friends from the Old Country, the conversation quickly went German. Especially when talking to Lisa Roderick, the mother of my best friend Kirk. Lisa had more to say, so I could faintly hear Lisa's voice on the receiver, with Mutti coming in now and then, "Yah, Lisel. Yah. Yah, naturlich (naturally). Nah, yah!" I've often wondered: Why didn't I ask her to teach me to speak German? At least I can say, "Yah!"

**How she tipped the taxi driver.** Mutti never drove, not even a golf cart, which would have helped when she played eighteen holes of golf at the Deauville Club. The Valley Cab Company took her everywhere she needed to go. She would pay the driver in cash and always added a little extra, saying as she handed him the money, "Und here is a little somezing extra for you, my deah."

One of Mutti's stops, every week, faithfully, was at the Valley Vista house, where I would be ready to jump into the cab and ride with her to church. My mother worked nights, slept days, so she never went with us.

The taxicab pulled up our driveway, I got in, and there was Mutti, nicely dressed, with a sweater, purse, and a rosary. After maybe a twenty-minute drive to St. Cyril's Catholic Church in Encino, we walked in together, dipped our fingers in the water, made the sign of the cross on forehead and shoulders, and sat in our usual place. This happened every Sunday morning, and even when I was at Kirk's house, the cab pulled up, and I jumped in.

The cab also came into play when I spent Wednesday nights at Mutti's house, on Dunbar Place, not far from my house. I ate schnitchel and watched *The Man From U.N.C.L.E.* on TV. So the next morning, the cab (without Mutti) would take me to elementary school.

Embarrassed, I tried to sneak from the parking lot to the classroom. Trying to be like Illya Kuryakin, Napoleon Solo's right-hand man from *U.N.C.L.E.*, I ducked through bushes and side-stepped along walls, a super-spy. But inevitably, it happened.

"Hey! YOU!"

Some kid caught the difference between me and the bush.

"HAY! Aren't you that kid that comes in a taxi?"

Humiliation! It would've been like being dropped off by a milkman, or in present day, maybe arriving on a doorstep, dropped there (and photographed) by the Amazon driver.

So when that happened, I just acted cool and nonchalant, paying no attention, just thinking about Illya and veener schnitchel. Casually, I sauntered into the fourth grade classroom.

Evenings at Mutti's house, weekends at her pool, and walking with her to Neff's Toys—all wonderful experiences, still vivid to this day. But I was not always a good boy. Especially at Neff's toy store.

"Oh, Mutti, will you buy it for me? Pleeeeeease?" I'd see some kind of toy, maybe a rocket ship, racing car set, or a robot, and man, I *really* wanted it. So I begged for it. Mutti couldn't resist. But she did put me through the paces.

"Deah, et iz not birsday."

"I know, Mutti, but..."

"It ez not Christmas."

"I know, Mutti, but..."

"Vat es ze occasion?"

Couldn't answer that one, so I just smiled, frowning at the same time. It didn't take long after that.

"Vell, I buy et for you."

The cab dropped me home, and I walked in with my present. My mother probably knew what had happened.

I think—well, I know—Mutti hid a very difficult part of her life. She never spoke of it. Neither did my mother, who also had a very difficult part of her life.

Really, I didn't know anything about Maria Koppl or Gertrude (Marguerite) Koppl or her brother my Uncle Werner, or Rudolph, my grandfather, who passed away when I was very little.

Much later in life, from other family members, I would hear the accounts of how Maria, Rudolph, Werner, and Gertrude came to the United States, fleeing from the incoming Nazis.

Or, maybe it's best that I didn't know. I'm not sure how I would have processed it, because later in life when I learned more, it was still quite a story to, as they say, wrap your mind around.

Perhaps my young life was spared that knowledge, while being served ordervers with Hawaiian Punch and a stir-stick with a whistle on it.

*A voice, an accent, a warm, delicious meal,*
*Our childhood memories, so vivid, so real.*

# Chapter 3
# CRUD STEAKS

THE 1957 THUNDERBIRD, WITH WHITE-WALL TIRES, AQUA-green paint job, hard-shell convertible top (with port hole) and back tail fins, pulled into the driveway.

My dad walked around the car and stepped up to the front door, ringing the doorbell. It wasn't my house, though, it was the home of Pauline and Cecil Jones who took care of me after school. I'd been expecting him, and I was excited.

He said he was coming by, which was unusual, and...he had a surprise.

Being about nine years old at the time, I'd asked a few brilliant, interrogative questions when talking to him on the phone the night before.

"What's the surprise, Dad?"

"What do you think it is?"

"A rocket ship?" I asked.

"Nope."

Now I was stumped. "A cake, maybe?"

"Not a cake."

So now, opening the door, and my dad standing there, my questions would finally be answered. He wasn't holding anything. Was it really small? Did he forget?

We walked out to the sports car. He opened the passenger door. I looked in.

Not a rocket ship and definitely not a cake.

It was a guy.

A person—like a teenager—with short curly hair, glasses, and a T-shirt. He could have been in the movie *American Graffitti*, except it hadn't been made yet.

Dad said, "This is your brother."

Stumped again. No certificate to prove it, but I knew I did *not* have a brother.

I mean, you know, I would have seen him around the house, right?

His name was Mark, and he was my half-brother, from my dad's first marriage to Mark's mother, Florence. Soon after I met him, Mark married Bonnie Kern, August 21, 1965, at St. Cyril's in Encino, and for the next many years, Mark and Bonnie would come to the Valley Vista house, pick me up, and give me a wonderful weekend adventure.

And it started the very first time their dark green Mustang drove up the driveway.

But it was a bit of an awkward start.

They weren't awkward, but I was a quiet, introverted boy, and just sat there in the backseat, silent. Probably a little nervous, a little embarrassed, and a little out of the world of my room and my toys. Then a voice broke the quietness.

Bonnie: "Boy, Roddy sure is being quiet back there."

Mark: "Geez, are you sure we didn't leave him on the porch?"

Bonnie, after turning around, "Nope. He's back there. He's breathing."

"Okay, Roddy," Mark said, "you can take the football out of your mouth now."

That did it. I burst out laughing. I pushed the laugh down, but it kept popping up. Because I could see it: a football popping out of my mouth. *FFFF-POP!*

It was the funniest thing anyone had ever said to me.

Gradually, I calmed down and resumed being embarrassed.

But that was a pivotal point—my entire life tipped in a new direction, from timid to tickled, from frigid to funny. Many years of laughter and good times with Mark and Bonnie successfully broke Roddy out of his shell. From yokes to jokes, folks!

Because, hands down, my brother and his wife were the funniest people I knew. For example:

**Funny names.** Mark seldom called people by their names. Their normal names. Instead, he made up names. I was Uncle Tonoose (from *The Danny Thomas Show*), Toad Butler, Screw-loose, Miserable Swine, or Louie Dah Louse. Bonnie was George, Haggus Baggus, or Atilla the Hun. Who else did that? Nobody!

**Crud steaks and super potatoes.** Bonnie could cook, so that was a new experience for me. But instead of meat and potatoes, she made what Mark called "crud steaks and super potatoes." He described them as hamburger patties mashed through by football cleats. This meal came with peaches too. Mmmmm.

**Drive-in movies.** Mark would invite Kirk to come along as we went to the drive-in theater, where you parked to face an outdoor movie screen and speaker boxes were clamped to partially rolled-down windows. We always stopped to pick up a bucket of

Kentucky Fried Chicken, which seemed to mostly stay in the back seat with me and Kirk.

**Re-voicing TV shows.** Kicked back and comfy, Mark and I would turn down the sound on the TV and redo the voices. Sci-fi movies were the best...The timid soldier made his way through the underground tunnel, approaching the aliens, probably bug-eyed and lizard-skinned. Normally he'd say, "This is the army. Surrender!" Now he said (one of us said), "I've got a large pizza for a Mr. Zeltzenheimer. Would that be you?" We often rolled off the bed, laughing.

**Human training wheels.** At some point they found out I was terrible at sports. Mark taught me to throw a frisbee, which meant he threw it directly to me and I lobbed it out into the weeds or the woods. To my shock, they gave me a ten-speed bike for Christmas, and I had to admit, at ten or eleven years old, I couldn't ride a bicycle. Enter Mark the Human Training Wheels, as he ran along with me, behind the bike, holding on somehow, keeping me upright and going somewhat straight ahead. Eventually he let go. And I did fine. Fine with falling included.

Mark and Bonnie also went to Mass and took me with them, of course. Afterward we went to Dupar's restaurant for pancakes. Or to Bonnie's mom and dad's apartment for more eggs and bacon than I'd ever seen in my life. Before every meal, Mark said grace, the traditional Catholic food blessing, but recited at lightning-speed, yet with every word clearly pronounced. Amazing.

Things only got better when Jennifer and Jaime were born, and I got a new name, not Mark-Butlerized yet beloved: Uncle Roddy.

In turn, I gave the girls their own Uncle Roddy-ized names: Juniper and Jomre. Sometimes we still use those names. Smile.

When I came for a visit, I was in charge of bedtime stories. Yes, a chance to put my newfound humor skills to work! My imagination flew off the rails...

It was the same old story each time. There was a countdown—an endless countdown—as I lit the pretend fuse attached to the pretend dynamite. To power the pretend spaceships. The fuse kept sputtering and going out, until—unexpectedly—*KA-BOOMIE!*

Imagine giggling little girl noises here.

Our spaceships rocketed into pretend outer space. Except that our spaceships were pretend trashcans (NASA authorized trashcans, of course), and the flights were very, *very* bumpy, all of us bouncing all over the bed.

I'm not sure we ever landed on a pretend planet. It was all a bounce-fest after that.

Did this lull them to sleep?

No, and Bonnie would always arrive to end the stories, shoo me out the door, and click off the light.

> *What's so funny about funny? It's what you see and hear.*
> *Funny brings out sunny, shining light and love and cheer.*

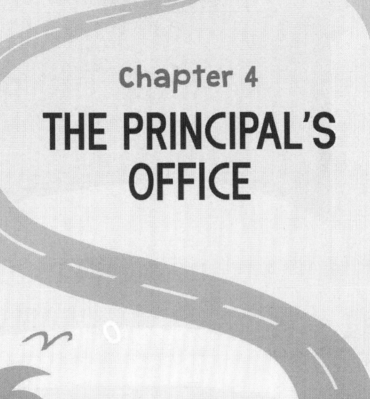

Chapter 4

# THE PRINCIPAL'S OFFICE

SIX YEARS IN ELEMENTARY SCHOOL, AND WHERE DID I FIND myself? In the principal's office.

Back then in elementary school, in the 1960s, a trip to the principal's office could mean a few words of advice, a stern lecture, or at worst, what the British call "smack-bottom." You know. A spanking by hand or paddle. No telling how many smacks on the poor bottom.

But I didn't worry about any of that because it was the last day of school, and I had graduated, a sixth grader at Swanson's Ranch School in sunny Southern California. I even had a trophy with a gold plastic cup and shiny plaque displaying the years I had attended. It said:

RODERICK BUTLER
1961–67

I didn't know if I did something outstanding within those years or was awarded for normalcy. But, hey, who else had a trophy for simply being there? Not perfect attendance, just regular existence.

Swanson's was what they called a private school—private as in not a public school. The ranch-style location had horse stables at the very back and was next to a riding rink, a large playground, then the one-story classrooms, and the front parking lot, where Illya stepped out of the taxicab.

The dirt ground of the playground hurt, especially when you fell on it, thrown down to the hard surface. Nobody knocked me down—I threw myself down, and though it hurt, it was part of the act. As far back as third grade, Roddy was a performer.

Blame it on Micky, Mike, Peter, and Davy...the Monkees. You know, the popstars that tried to rival the Beatles and had their own TV show.

The Monkees introduced me to that wonderful part of life: music. Their hit "I'm a Believer" echoed in my mind and played on the suitcase-style record player in my room. I tapped my knees to the beat—the first clue to my internal drummer—hoping for sticks and a drum kit.

So there on the playground, me and my friend Gary performed "I'm a Believer," hoping our audience would believe we were even a little bit like the Monkees. Yeah, it was hard to believe, since Gary played an electric guitar without an amplifier, without a pic, which sounded more like fingernails on a washtub than anything musical. With my drumsticks—I mean unsharpened pencils—I kept the beat—on an old cardboard shoebox. Gary sang. Sort of.

Yes, we drew a small crowd, there on the dirt, mostly first, second, and third graders.

The song didn't last long, so after that I did my "stand-up" routine. Which involved more falling down than standing up.

"I won't fall down," I'd say, sitting on a wooden bench. "I'm sitting here, comfortable and safe. Why would I fall down?" I milked that for all it was worth, and inevitably, I lounged back on the backless bench and threw myself to the dirt, landing with an *OOOMPH!*

I got laughs, though it took several "smack-backs" to get there.

But standing in the gymnasium, with all the parents and grandparents attending on the last day of school, I was a nervous, bashful kid about to receive my award for being there.

I heard my name echo against the walls and stepped forward to get the little trophy.

In a few minutes, graduation concluded and the school year was over! My mother and I were heading to the car when she decided, I guess, to thank Mr. and Mrs. Swanson. And you know where they were to be found.

In the principal's office. Just those words struck fear in my heart.

But there was really no reason to worry, because my mother was with me. Everyone knew that Mr. and Mrs. Swanson were super nice. Much nicer than the sixth grade math teacher. Mrs....never mind.

My mother was friends with the Swansons, and since my mom enjoyed talking, I had settled in for a long winter. I mean, summer. In the principal's office.

Mildred Swanson was also talkative, but her husband, Leonard, who looked like a cross between John Wayne and an insurance salesman, was more the quiet type. That said, I was surprised when he moseyed over to me and asked me a question. Especially considering I was already on summer vacation. I hoped it wasn't a math question.

He pointed to a stack of books on the coffee table. In particular he pointed to a large book with gold-leafed pages and a dark, rippled cover. Mr. Swanson placed a hand on the book and asked me if I knew what it was. Of course I did. I was a good Catholic, and I'd seen a Bible many times. Not this close, but still, that was a no-brainer. I figured everybody knew what a Bible looked like.

The big problem, though, was, how did he get it? Priests had Bibles, nuns probably had Bibles, but I didn't know anybody else was allowed to have one. Right there on the coffee table. Not sitting on an ornate podium or behind protective glass.

Wait. Mr. Swanson? Could he be...a notorious Bible thief disguised as a mild-mannered school principal? No way!

I probably saw the Bible-police with blazing sirens chasing Mr. Swanson's car as he sped away from the Smithsonian—one hand on the wheel, the other steadying a rare, golden-fleeced Bible on the seat next to him. But this scene was quickly swiped away by his soft voice asking, "Roddy, do you know what this is?"

Feeling intimidated—in spite of my incredible trophy—I didn't answer. So he answered, "This is the Bible. It's full of the greatest stories you could ever read." Not what I expected him to say.

Stories? I love stories! But to be honest, when the priest read from the Bible during Mass, it was pretty boring. The only priest that held my attention was Father Tellers, who always opened the sermon with a reading from *Peanuts* by Charles Shultz.

Anyway. Mr. Swanson didn't open the Bible or give me a Bible or anything like that. The time in the principal's office quickly came to a close, and we drove away, taking me into the joys of an endless summer vacation.

> *A table, a book with an en-goldened shine,*
> *And a glance far ahead to a golden time.*

# Chapter 5

# STRANGE CLOTHES

THAT ENDLESS SUMMER VACATION CAME TO A SCREECHING halt when I opened my closet.

Like any normal summer day, I looked inside to find a T-shirt to wear. Anything that would go with my jeans, which was everything. Strangely, amongst the brightly colored tees was something else. Something unwanted, unneeded.

Too much of something unwanted and unneeded. A row of starched, short-sleeved shirts with buttons and collars. And worst of all, they were khaki. You know, that bland color somewhere between yellow, brown, and yuck. And all of them—exactly the same.

Lo and behold—my military school uniforms.

Shirts and pants. And a khaki hat, floppy, something like a milk-man's hat, only not bright and cheerful—no—just khaki.

Too soon, the months evaporated, and a wood-paneled station wagon entered our driveway with a bump and a bounce, then beeped the horn. It looked like a cross between a car, a bus, and a boat. The driver's door swung open. I stood in my doorway.

A lady named Mrs. Pelka got out and motioned me to get in.

I walked out in stiff, starchy military clothes, with shiny shoes, little brass shields on my collar, and the floppy hat slipped through my belt. I carried a thing called a briefcase, a little bit like the *Man from U.N.C.L.E.* toy attaché case, but completely without plastic weapons or tracking devices. And of course, no radio communi-cator disguised as a fountain pen.

Junior high school, here I come.

There were other boys in the station wagon, all wearing the same uniform. Cadets, we were called. We had short hair and shiny belt buckles. And black nameplates with white lettering pinned to the top flap of the right shirt pocket. Our names were printed in un-fun lettering, last names only. So there I was. BUTLER. Anyone could look at my shirt and know my name. My last name, anyway. At least they didn't spell it with two T's.

Military school. We marched in formation. Stood at attention. Marched to the mess hall and ate the food. And the food? It was pretty good, really. We joked about "mystery meat" and powdered eggs, but the milk in the little cartons was cold and delicious.

Another benefit was building close friendships. I met Josh Ketcham in Mrs. Pelka's station wagon, and later made friends with Nelson Brazeau and Brad Strathearn. (We would all go to military high school too. Oops. Spoilers!)

There was something about finding friends in the world of uniforms, short haircuts, and name tags. Lasting relationships were forged, like irons in the fire. And what was the sign of a real friend-ship, there in military school? You called each other by first names. I had many first-name friends.

I attended Ridgewood Military Academy from 1968 to 1970. I'm not really sure why I was there. Maybe because my single-parent mom wanted male role models in my life or more discipline or to continue my private school education. The discipline was there, for sure.

So I stayed busy being good, doing the right thing (not the wrong thing), because I did not—repeat—did *not* want to get a "swat." A real smack-bottom with a wooden paddle. Mr. Swanson did not exist here; we had Colonel Metcalf and Lieutenant Wooley, and the latter especially meant business. I found out. The hard way.

At Ridgewood I realized what I already suspected. I was terrible at sports but good at funny faces. And funny voices. But try to throw a football, make a layup, or kick any kind of ball—it's just not gonna happen.

Still, physical fitness was mandatory, and one day I found myself waiting to rotate into the volleyball game. Bored, I guess, I tossed a rock out into some grass. Well, it was a terrible toss, and the rock flew upwards at the perfect trajectory/velocity to strike an exterior dorm lightbulb that shattered to pieces. The game stopped. Everybody turned. And there was BUTLER. Master of destruction.

On my way to Lieutenant Wooley's office, I wondered if I should consider a career as a major league baseball pitcher. Or an electrician. Well, I didn't think any of that, really. I was in mortal dread of the paddle. And I experienced it.

First off, I had to remove my wallet and my floppy hat. More bottom for the smack.

The actual swat was preceded by several trial swats, where he jokingly practiced his aim, coming around gently and doing a touch-bottom. Then, after a few of those—*KA-POWIE!* A swat worth remembering. To this very day.

This nicely kept campus, nestled in Woodland Hills, had students from first through ninth grades—all kinds of kids, from all kinds of homes. The first year, I attended as a day student. But in the second and third years, I boarded there, Monday through Friday.

Welcome to dormitory life. Nothing like my room at home, with my bed, my models, and my music. Instead: Stiff bunks, shared bathrooms, new kinds of smells, and the military way, reflected in polished insignia, belt buckles, how you folded your underclothes, and the making of the bed—tight enough to bounce a quarter back into the air.

Student leaders tried too hard to show their power. They could make you stand at attention for as long as they wanted and give you demerits if you didn't cooperate. And I guess I was a sheltered child, because I was shocked when I heard nasty words—some I recognized plus some new ones.

It was a rude slice of life in many ways, although there were fun times too. And all of it played out against the audio backdrop of 1960s rock-and roll-music, sounding fresh and tinny and wild in my ear bud—just one ear bud—attached by a wire to my transistor radio.

And that radio was set to the one and only 93 KHJ Boss Radio. Great DJ's kept that music rockin' and rollin', names I've never forgotten, like The Real Don Steele, Robert W. Morgan, and my favorite, Wolfman Jack. I can still hear them. Even without the ear bud.

I said I didn't know why I was there because I didn't, but the Higher Up did. Indeed, it was part of a higher plan. A better, brighter plan.

I believe God always has a plan for our lives, though he is not obligated to tell us the details of it. Or the timing. We have to trust him. But I didn't know any of that back then.

Although I'm pretty sure I had one or two guardian angels with me, helping me not get hit by stray baseball pitches or the punches of student bullies. And, at the campus pool, making that one kid stop when he was holding my head underwater, almost to the panic-point.

And another time, helping Nelson to remember to come get me when the bugle call summoned us to report for dinner. I was out in the far yard, near the volleyball court and the music building, strapped to the chin-up bars.

It wasn't torture. It was my own stupidity. I had read the story of the famous escape artist Harry Houdini and thought I could do a similar kind of handcuff release trick. Didn't have handcuffs, so with Nelson's reluctant help, I lashed myself to the horizontal bar with ropes, and after he left, wiggled every which way to get out. It wasn't going to happen. The sun was slowly going down. And nobody had cell phones yet. Or any reason to head out to the back part of the school.

But then, as the song goes, "Along Comes Nelson"—not "Mary"— probably realizing I was still out there, strung up and stupid.

It was good to see him walking toward me. I was getting hungry.

> *The former days, the tender tide.*
> *Angels watching on either side.*

# Chapter 6

# HOME FOR THE WEEKEND

Being away at school all week made coming home really special.

On Friday afternoons at Ridgewood's front parking lot, I'd be standing there with my briefcase. A car would pull up. It was my mom or a friend of hers, who would drive me across the San Fernando Valley to Sherman Oaks. And there, finally, under the palm trees, was Valley Vista Boulevard, and home.

I walked to the front door, smelling gardenias, and into the living room, with the plastic-covered couch and chairs, into the hallway, and made a sharp right turn. Ahhh.

My room. And the stuff in my room: more spaceship models, more sci-fi books, and especially, more vinyl record albums. From listening to 93 KHJ and their "Boss Thirty," I got to know different groups and artists. I'd come a long way from the Monkees. Music became like a familiar friend, and I especially liked listening for the drums.

I'd learned to play the snare drum at Ridgewood. I joined the Drum and Bugle Corps, making stick music with the other drummers and the guy pounding clock-steady rhythm on the bass drum against his chest. But my heart went beat-beat-beat to the sounds of rock n' roll.

The Doors had a cool, mysterious sound. The Moody Blues sounded like their name. Three Dog Night had three amazing lead singers, plus great instruments with Floyd Sneed on drums. Jethro Tull featured a maniac flute player, who made the flute as cool n' gritty as any electric guitar. And of course: the Beatles, the Beach Boys, Simon and Garfunkel, and the good old Monkees. I didn't sing along, but I knew the words to all of their hits. And all of the drum riffs, which I patted out on my knees.

Kirk and I got together, enjoying our Hot Wheels, Major Matt Mason figures, and models from our favorite science fiction TV shows. About that time we started making our own monster movies with his Super 8 camera.

Some weekends were spent with Mark and Bonnie, some with Josh Ketcham and his friends, and some just me and my mom, often eating at the Jolly Roger at Bullock's Fashion Square in Sherman Oaks. I'd eat while she talked, then go run around to the different stores, coming back about the time she was finished. Several years later, I'd return to one of those stores to purchase a hand puppet. But never mind about that.

Some weekends included a visit to Mutti's pool, with its clear, blue water, surrounding walls of shrubbery, and outdoor table with an umbrella in the middle. But this idyllic setting held a strong, disturbing, yet victorious memory for me. It involves my little self, reaching for a pool toy that was a little too far away. I later captured it in a poem...

## Bubbling Downward

Afternoon at Mutti's
Large and beautiful pool
And I'm
Bubbling downward,
Looking left, right,
Water everywhere

Watching the concrete pool wall
Moving upward as I
Roddy Butler,
Age two or three
Bubble downward,
Sinking in
Mutti's beautiful pool.
Okay. Drowning, but too little to know it.
Watching the stubbled white wall
Of the pool
Go up and up and up and
Wondering why, not understanding
I was going down...down...down...
Until
*KER-SPLASH!*
Here comes Doris Waller
Bubbling downward!
My godmother plunges into pool water
In her regular clothes and all
To rescue
Her sweet little godson who
Reached over the concrete edge
To grab his favorite floaty toy
And tumble into family history.
In two short strokes Dodo
Scoops me up and
Like a rocket,
Breaks the surface and
Brings her startled little aquanaut
Safely back to air and light and

Even his favorite floaty toy.
And only this moment
Do I realize I had experienced
My first plunge into the idea of
SALVATION.
*(Written 1988)*

It's hard to top that story, but...one Saturday morning, I walked from Valley Vista to the record store on Ventura, passing a house that caught my attention. I heard beautiful piano music wafting into the air. It grew as I passed by the living room window, where—without staring or being obvious—I noticed a pretty lady playing a grand piano. That made an impression.

I launched a hope heavenward that some day I might have a house like that, and a lady like that, and "live" classical piano music like that. I think heaven was listening. Well, I know it. But again, spoilers.

Sunday nights I had to return to Ridgewood—or "The Rock" as Mark called it—duffle bag and briefcase in hand. I'd be dropped off at the front of school, then made my way back to the dorm, opening the front door to the long hallway ahead, lined by door-ways to cadets' rooms, usually three boys to a room. The door had a particular closing sound, with a cadence of squeaky hinges followed by the big boom of the door slamming closed. Something like:

**Dutt—Dutt—Dutt—Eeeeeaaaa—Ka-Baam!**

After Tapps (the bugle call for "You guys go to sleep!"), we cadets would hear that sound play its mechanical music as Lieutenant Wooley left the dorm and walked a two-minute walk to his bungalow quarters on campus. Once there he would switch on the intercom system that allowed him to hear the slightest cadet-made noise within the dorm. However...

Within those two minutes, the listening system was off, which meant you could do anything you wanted to do. Run down the hallway with a pillow to bap somebody on the head, do your best exotic bird-call impressions, or sneak into the hallway, which was usually polished enough that you could get a running start and slide pretty far, like a skater, in bare socks, passing room after room.

I should not have done this, but...once I heard the final *BAAM*, I crept neatly into the hallway, ready to cause some kind of mischief, not sure what kind.

I was about three doorways down when the light snapped on. I turned.

There he was. Lieutenant Wooley. In some kind of brilliant ex-military maneuver, he had allowed the door to close while he himself stayed inside the dorm, waiting like a panther. And smiling like one, when he said, very proud of himself, "BUTLER? What do you think you're doing?"

The story does not end in a swat; it ends on the moon. At least, that's what the hallway wall looked like to me as I stood there for an hour, my nose to the wall, and the blurred surface of that wall having a sedating, fanciful, almost lunar glow. Not really. Really I kept hearing his voice. What *did* I think I was doing?

Oh well, what's an hour at the wall, with dorm friends walking by, giggling behind my back? Or some going by, like Nelson, really feeling sorry for me?

*The up and the down and the slide,*
*All the memories we've carried inside.*
*To a good friend, we often confide,*
*As consolation strengthens our stride.*

Chapter 7

# MY FRIEND
# THE OCEAN

One of my best friends is the ocean.

She has played a recurring role in the story of my life. Her tide moving in at different times, in different places. Then slipping away, only to return, farther down the coastline. Then sweeping out again, leaving memories glistening on the shore:

My dad had a sailboat.

My brother Mark followed suit, boating at the yacht club.

Me, in my childhood days at Waikiki Beach, Honolulu, Hawaii, listening to the pounding surf while my mother snored in the hotel room.

With a splash I remember the diving bell breaking the water and submerging, with Kirk and me inside it, at Pacific Ocean Park—POP—an amusement park in Santa Monica. Down, down, down...then up-splashing into daylight.

Another splash sends me *Twenty Thousand Leagues Under the Sea*, and then to a television ocean for *Sea Hunt* and a *Voyage to the Bottom of the Sea*.

———

But from 1971 to 1973, the ocean waves were pounding onto the beach in Carlsbad, California, at my high school, Army and Navy Academy (ANA): "Where the campus meets the surf."

Yes, another military school.

ANA was about an hour and a half from Los Angeles. Several of my friends from Ridgewood were there, so that was nice. But this was a true boarding school. We only went home for Thanksgiving, Christmas, and summer vacation.

So across the school year, these were the images of my life: my dorm room, roommate, footlocker, desk, window, posters of The Doors and The Moody Blues, clothing rack, and the upper bunk in which I slept. This small room was home.

But the school had a sprawling feel to it, with spacious lawns terracing downward to the beach. The presence of the ocean was always in the air, and its rushing, colliding waves always in the background, punctuated by cackling sea gulls.

The long white dormitory buildings stood in U-shaped formations, with rows of green-painted doors. The indoor basketball court doubled as an auditorium, with a wooden-planked theatrical stage fronted by deep blue curtains. That stage, and the world of theater, I would come to love.

I still couldn't do a layup, swing a bat, or throw a pass, but I could swim, so I did that, with the floating divider ropes keeping me in the correct lane. Fortunately, I swam in the right direction. And knew to turn around when I came to the edge of the pool. It would have been embarrassing if I had paddled up out of the pool and toward the bleachers. But there were other problems.

As I swam, Coach Dan would call out, "Butler! Kick your feet! Use your feet!" Problem was, if I kicked with my feet, my arms would forget what they were supposed to do. That problem didn't show up so much when I played water polo, but I did, one time, get "swum over" by a guy from the other team barreling over my head and onward, kicking bubbles in my face.

It's funny how things in your life (kind of like bubbles) rise to the surface, without you making that happen or even thinking about it.

I'm thinking of ideas, interests, talents, desires. Pursuits. Aspirations to be involved in things that become a major part of your life, even if no one specifically told you to consider them. For me, I could never be separated from this crazy desire to write stories. I grew up with movies and imaginative TV shows. Books, toys, music, artwork. And, wiggling its way to the top, always near the top: humor.

And so in high school, often unrelated to studies or sports or activities, people somehow gravitate to others like themselves. For example, funny people find other funny people. And there's not even a Funny Club you join to meet them. Paths just somehow...cross.

I remember walking down the outside hallway of a dorm, passing windows of the individual rooms, and hearing this interesting music—classical, yet catchy. (I love classical music now but didn't know anything about it back then.) The instruments were not normal, but more electric, or specifically—*electronic*.

Eventually, I met the cadet who lived in that room, Greg Shannon. I also met an album called *Switched-On Bach,* leading me to the discovery of electronic music and, later, Moog Synthesizers. Greg became a great friend, and we went on to create our own synthesizer, winning an award at the Nineteenth Annual Greater San Diego Science Fair.

Around that time, I heard about Masque & Wig, the drama troupe at the Academy. I'd never been involved in drama, except that I'd been involved with it my entire life, just not under that name. So...

BUTLER went to an audition. In a classroom. He met Mr. Carden, a teacher, and the head of the drama department. That's not all that happened.

BUTLER landed the part of Charlie Brown in *You're a Good Man, Charlie Brown*. Then he played Felix Unger in *The Odd Couple* and had a role in *Billy Budd* as an old-timer named O'Daniel.

Then BUTLER met the student president of Masque & Wig, (Brian) HORNER. And once again, Funny met Funny. And it was pretty funny.

Brian was a talented actor and a really nice guy, a year ahead of me in school. We became fast friends.

Like me, he loved Laurel and Hardy, aka Stan and Ollie. He had the expressive eyes for Oliver Hardy; I had the chin for Stan Laurel. Together, in Masque & Wig, we did our own mini-play, *Here We Come A-bumbling*, based on their most famous routines. The applause rang out, proving that great comedy is timeless and, even if interpreted by young actors, can bring down the house, as they say.

Somehow, we were able to capture their expressions and voices and come close to that wonderful timing that allowed them to light up the silver screen. One of our favorite skits was the scene where Stan and Ollie, as sailors, try to treat two lady friends to sodas. The only problem: they have enough money for three sodas but not four. Ollie quietly tells Stan they'll split their soda. When it arrives, Ollie says, "Go ahead and drink your half." Stan takes a long, long, long sip...that drains the glass. Ollie, a man without a soda, stares at him, bringing Stan to the verge of tears.

OLLIE: Do you know what you've done?

STAN: I couldn't help it.

OLLIE: Why?

STAN:...My half was on the bottom!

Brian and I had all kinds of running gags, from confused news announcers to incredibly brilliant people totally misunderstanding each other, and random voice impressions of rock stars and movie actors.

We had lots of laughter, and none of the class awareness of him being a senior and me a junior. He did have his own cottage, and I was in the dorm, but it didn't matter. The friendship was solid.

However, there was something about him I couldn't put my finger on. A kind of difference.

He didn't do drugs or swear or hurt people or cheat or anything. But it went beyond those kinds of things. Okay, maybe that's the word.

There was something *beyond* about Brian Horner. I knew he was one of the "Jesus people," or the stronger term, "Jesus freaks," but he didn't act like a preacher or a pushy religious person. None of the "holier than thou" stuff. Of course, he didn't have long hair or beads or anything—this was military school, and we all looked alike.

Especially when seen from a distance, like when parents and families came to attend a parade. From their view, out in the bleachers, we must have looked like identical toy soldiers.

So it was really something when somebody truly stood out, not in a bad way, but in a good way.

I didn't ask him about his faith. He wasn't Catholic, I didn't think, because he wasn't with us Catholic cadets when we marched to church for Mass on Sunday mornings. (Did I miss Mutti's cab ride days? Yes.) We felt like GI Joe action figures, stopping at the front of the church, then "falling out" of ranks and entering the church.

I wondered, *What was it about Horner? What made him different?* I didn't ask him; we just had fun being funny. Then one night, he told me.

*In the course of normal days,*
*The Spirit moves in hidden ways.*
*In a word, a thought, a choice,*
*Suddenly: The Still Small Voice.*

# Chapter 8
# THE BELLY OF THE BOAT

*BILLY BUDD* WAS THE LAST PLAY OF THE YEAR. HORNER LANDED the lead role: Billy Budd.

A large-scale wooden sailing ship was built upon the Academy stage, with a cyclorama sky behind it. Amazing, really, especially for high school. The show was soon to open; these were the last few rehearsals, scheduled in the evening.

I played O'Daniel, an old sailor, and I had one of my dad's old pipes and my Irish accent ready to go.

We were down in the belly of the ship, below the stage, waiting for our cues. Somebody would call down when our scene was coming up.

So we had a little time to talk. Somehow the name Jesus came into the conversation. Horner said he wanted to ask me a few questions —would that be okay? And I said sure. It went like this:

HORNER: Butler, do you have Jesus in your heart?

I had to pause on that one. I'd never heard it said that way.

BUTLER: I go to Mass and receive Holy Communion, so I'm pretty sure I do.

HORNER: Okay, but if you're not totally sure—100 percent sure —then you don't.

He explained that it was one of those things you know, like knowing that the sun had come up, because it's shining brightly, warming you up. Or knowing that the rain is pouring down all around you, and you're soaked. *You know that you know.* I was chewing on that little phrase when he continued.

HORNER: Have you ever prayed and asked Jesus into your heart?

BUTLER: I don't think I've ever prayed those exact words. But I've prayed the Our Father and the Hail Mary lots of times.

This next thing he said blew me away. I've remembered it for fifty years!

HORNER: Butler, look. It's like this. It's not about religion. It's about *relationship*.

BUTLER: What do you mean?

HORNER: In the Bible, in Revelation 3:20, Jesus said, "Behold, I stand at the door and knock: if any man hear my voice, and open the door, I will come in to him, and sup with him, and he with me." Sup means like having dinner with somebody. Jesus wants to be your friend. He wants to have a relationship with you, Butler. He wants to be your personal Lord and Savior.

BUTLER: (stunned silence)

I'd never heard anything like that. It didn't sound Catholic, but it didn't sound anti-Catholic either. I figured if all this was really from the Bible, I should pay attention to it. The Bible was holy and truthful, and I was sure that priests and Catholics would agree with the Bible, even though all of this was very new.

I was holding O'Daniel's pipe, trying to think it all through. Then he continued.

HORNER: Do you believe you are a sinner?

BUTLER: Um, yeah, I believe that. I guess. I mean, what is a sinner?

We sat together in the shadows, keeping an eye on the lit opening above us, the ladder that went up into it, and listening for the voice that would call us to skedaddle. I remember the smell of fresh lumber around us and the faint, familiar scent from my dad's old pipe, mixing into the newness of what I was hearing.

Brian explained how the Bible said that all people have sinned, but Christ died to take our sins away. And to put Christ's work into effect—like cashing a check made out to me—I would need to pray a prayer. And the sinner's prayer was the thing to pray.

I didn't know that prayer, of course. But it all made sense to me.

The concept of having your sins forgiven, that I knew, from going to confession at St. Cyril's. I remember entering the confessional booth, closing the door, and sitting there in the dark. Then, with a kind of dragging, scratching sound, a small window would open to reveal a metal grate, or mesh, with the shadow of a man's head behind it.

I recited some words and then began to confess my sins to the priest. Trouble was, I couldn't think of any. So I told him that. From the other side, he said, softly, "Well, do you love your mother?" I said I did. He went on, "Do you love her enough?"

How did he know that? Well, I admitted, probably not, and he assigned me a number of prayers to pray, and it was over. I went out to a pew, knelt down, and got busy.

But this was something else. I was talking directly to the Lord, in my own words.

Horner said it was like laying out cards on a table, listing and confessing your sins, asking forgiveness, receiving forgiveness, and pledging trust in Jesus Christ as Lord and Savior.

I was trying to get this all straight in my mind when a shadow blocked the light above us and a voice called out, "Billy Budd, you're on in one minute!" Horner quickened his pace.

"You lay them out, all the sins you can think of, and all the others you might be forgetting too," he said. "The Bible says, 'All have sinned and fallen short of the glory of God.' To sin means to miss the mark. It's like, no matter how hard we try, no matter how good our aim is, we can never keep hitting a perfect bull's-eye. We can try to be good, but we can never live a perfect life that would be acceptable to a perfect God. So Jesus did that for us. The sacrifice of his sinless life purchased our forgiveness."

Now it *really* made sense. My heart, my mind, and my voice said, "What do I do?"

He said I should ask forgiveness and invite Jesus into my heart, making him my personal Lord and Savior. Then I should say, "In Jesus' name, amen." Then I would know for sure I was going to heaven.

That last statement hit me with a massive impact. The impact of something that could change the nature of every day after it.

Like swells in the ocean, Brian's words rolled over. And over.

Be sure I was going to heaven? I could be *sure* I was going to heaven? *Really?*

"Okay, gotta split!" Horner said and was up the ladder and gone.

Again I played it back. *I would know for sure I was going to heaven.* I decided to pray that prayer as soon as I got back to my dorm room.

My roommate at the time, "Doc" Hughes, was asleep on the lower bunk. I got ready for bed and quietly climbed up to the top bunk close to the ceiling. I sat up and prayed the prayer as Horner told me to, closing with "In Jesus' name, amen."

Nothing happened.

He didn't say that something *would* happen, but, well, I just thought there should be a feeling or a realization, or something kind of, um, holy, maybe.

Horner had also said that when I prayed the prayer, I would become a born-again Christian—that I'd be a new person, with a whole new life. I didn't feel any of that. What a disappointment.

Then I figured I might not have prayed it exactly as Horner instructed. Or that maybe God was busy answering more desperate prayers. That would make sense. Maybe I should be patient and wait in line, like at the airport.

I didn't know what to think, but faulting myself, I repeated the prayer and ended again with "In Jesus' name, amen."

Again, nothing. No life change, no born-again feelings.

*Well, I gave the Jesus relationship thing a try anyway,* I thought. *Too bad it didn't work. It's strange though. Horner's usually right about things.*

I turned over to go to sleep.

But before I drifted off, I heard a sentence in my head.

It was like a thought, but not the kind of thought I would think at the end of the day. It was like something you'd think in the morning, at the start of a new day. It was this:

"You've got a lot of work to do."

*Hmm. Weird,* I thought, and sailed off to sleep.

That was Monday, April 17, 1972.

> *Eternity sings in a second of time,*
> *All creation joins the silent rhyme.*
> *A symphonic prelude, a simple start,*
> *The curtains open to a waiting heart.*

Chapter 9

# THE NEXT MORNING

Before I describe April 18, 1972, I'd like to describe a similar new beginning.

When immigrants came to America, you would imagine they came with both expectations and uncertainties.

As they stepped off the boat, carrying their belongings and crossing the gangplank, setting foot on the new land, some were unsure, maybe even afraid. Some were ecstatic, thrilled to be entering a new world; others relieved to be delivered from difficult situations. Older people were moving slowly perhaps, younger people pushing ahead, parents stepping forward, their children following close behind them, the kids wide-eyed, taking it all in.

The experience of entering into faith, making a new commitment to Christ, is much like becoming a citizen of a new country.

To use New Testament terminology, it's like entering into a new kingdom. That entrance, taking that action, is, I believe, similar for all new believers.

But in terms of feelings and emotions, the experience can differ greatly from person to person. Some enter gradually, without much ceremony, growing up in a Christian home. Some come to the Lord from distressing situations, as some cadets did at the Academy, leaving behind drugs and addictions, even being suddenly freed from long-term habits. C.S. Lewis reportedly said he arrived kicking and screaming.

And some, like me, can recount a specific day and time they left a good—but maybe spiritually shallow—life to burst into a new day, a new morning, with Jesus Christ as Lord. Accompanied by a *rush* of feelings.

So then, I'm not saying that my experience should be like anyone else's experience, or that someone else is lacking if they didn't have the feelings I had on April 18, 1972.

But I do want to share these feelings with you—not just for this part of my journey, but all the other parts to follow—as they happened, with stumbling steps, mistakes, revelations, humor, and a few apologies. It's my story, and I'm not just sticking to it. I'm holding it close, and tight, with wonder and gratitude.

———

The next morning, I felt like I never came down from the top bunk. Not all the way to the linoleum floor anyway.

An ocean of goodness and glory swirled in my heart. I was very, very, very happy. I've never been high on drugs, but my heart was soaring. I've never been drunk, but I felt a kind of giddiness. Yet it was centered and deep—not blurring my vision or clouding my thinking. It was like all cloudiness had been swept away by a warm summertime breeze.

The sun was shining, bathing the campus in morning light. I was already dressed in my uniform with shoes, belt buckle, and insignia shined, and everything spiffy.

I had a spring in my step, but more than that—I felt like I was walking on air. Stepping along but without my shoes touching the pavement, the stairs, or the sidewalk to Horner's cottage.

I kept thinking, *Jesus is my Lord. Jesus is inside me. I'm a Christian— a born again Christian. Born. Again.* Like a baby coming out of a small, compacted space and birthed into a new kind of existence, something larger and more colorful. A place with new air in my lungs, new sights and sounds all around me.

I arrived, knocked on the green door, and went in. I still remember my words.

BUTLER: Horner, I'm going to have to beat you up.

HORNER: Okay. What time did you get up?

BUTLER: About half an hour ago.

HORNER: I was up earlier, so I guess I beat *you* up.

BUTLER: I'm going to beat you up for not telling me about Jesus sooner!

I walked through my normal schedule that day but was very preoccupied. *Okay, I actually have Jesus Christ alive inside of me. The real, actual, living, biblical Jesus. He is not the marble statue I saw in church, still on a cross. He is not just the name you read on a page. He is not just the person who lived 2,000 years ago. Wait—he did live 2,000 years ago, of course—but he is also alive and well today and answered my knock, took away my sins, and came into my heart-house, where he is, RIGHT NOW.*

And then: *Man, I feel so alive. I hope I'm not glowing. But this is amazing, incredible. How will I tell my mom? Mutti? My friends? Will they believe me? I mean, has this happened to anyone else at ANA? Besides me and Horner? Has it happened to anyone else in the world? I mean, if somebody else had Jesus Christ in their heart like I did, that would be on the front page of the LA Times, right? Walter Cronkite would talk about it on national news. It would be history making. It would be a miracle! What if Horner and I were the only two born-again Christians on earth? That would be so...weird!*

Like an immigrant having passed through Ellis Island, I was taking my first-ever steps into a brave new world.

And speaking of steps, I had a hard decision to make. The beginning of many such difficult decisions. This one: Where do I go Sunday morning? Do I march to Catholic Church as I had before? For some reason, I didn't want to. I wasn't against the idea, or against my Catholic background, but I wondered if there would be something more like what I had discovered, something that would tie into this newness in my life.

One of the other new Christians at ANA told me about a church they liked, something with the word *Tabernacle* in it. And I think the word *Gospel*. Those sounded good to me, so that next Sunday, I marched with a different group of cadets—not as many—to a normal looking, everyday church, with a steeple and stain glass windows.

Except that I'd never been to another type of church. Ever.

We broke ranks and walked like normal people (in uniforms) into the sanctuary. It was different! Very different!

People were standing up at the front with musical instruments. No crucifix and none of the other things I expected were up at the front. The pews were the same, but along the walls I didn't see the statues of Stations of the Cross. Kind of missed seeing that.

The service began, with a man in a suit and tie greeting us, speaking into a microphone that was mounted on a tall cabinet-like thing, which, though I didn't know it, was a pulpit. *What's that for?* I wondered.

The music kicked in, and it was nice. Organ, piano, and people singing. Songs I'd never heard before, but they were pleasant, and I heard the name Jesus several times.

Then the leader, of course, the pastor, walked over to the tall cabinet-thing, opened it from behind, and pulled out...tah dah! A saxophone. He started playing along, and I had my answer. *Of course, that's where all the leaders keep their saxophones!*

At night, on the top bunk, my face not far from the ceiling, I'd fall asleep, feeling both contentment and jubilation. I'd say, softly—or whisper—"I love you, Lord Jesus." And I knew, somehow, across time and space, through dimensions or galaxies or somewhere above the sky, he heard me, and impressed my heart with comfort, as if he'd said, "I love you too."

> *Feelings are fragile, are fickle, are true, but*
> *How do I navigate these new feelings from you?*
> *Of Spirit, of wind-gust, of fountain, or rock?*
> *How do I express it, when I cannot even talk?*

# Chapter 10
# NEW LIFE

YES, IT WAS OFFICIAL. I WAS A JESUS PERSON NOW.

Not just a good person, or a person who wanted to avoid getting a swat. I wanted to live my life for Christ.

That was my new main thing. Right up there with being funny. Well, above that, ha ha.

My walk with Jesus and my new perspectives on life and eternal life were what really mattered. It all made so much sense. Life made sense. It seemed to have order and purpose.

That was good news, and I wanted to pass it on. That should be easy, right? I'll just tell others what Horner told me, right? I was ready. Let's do this thing!

But I really wasn't ready. Telling others, or witnessing—effectively —turned out to be more difficult than I imagined. Thankfully, especially in my baby-Christian days, I had help.

We had these things called tracts. These were small, hand-sized booklets that explained the gospel, often with cartoons or diagrams.

One of these, maybe the best, was *The Four Spiritual Laws* by an outstanding Christian leader and writer, Dr. Bill Bright. (At first, I couldn't believe his name was really Bill Bright, which sounded like a name right out of the Marvel universe, but that was his name.) And he did shine brightly, like a superhero, through his organization Campus Crusade for Christ, and across the eighty-two years of his life on this planet.

One page in his tract really impacted me.[1]

Self-Directed Life

**S** - Self is on the
throne
**†** - Christ is outside
the life
**●** - Interests are directed by
self, often resulting in
discord and frustration

Christ-Directed Life

**†** - Christ is in the life
and on the throne
**S** - Self is yielding to Christ
**●** - Interests are directed
by Christ, resulting in
harmony with God's
plan

The diagram, shown above, featured two circles.

Inside the Self-Directed Life circle was a random arrangement of things: Self on the throne; Christ outside the life; and Interests directed by self, often resulting in discord and frustration. Not good.

Inside the Christ-Directed Life was an organized arrangement of things: Christ in the life and on the throne; Self de-throned, yielding to Christ; and Interests directed by Christ, resulting in harmony with God's plan. Very, very good.

I loved the musicality of that term, "in harmony with God's plan." What a goal. Thank you, Dr. Bright, for an explanation of the Christian life, so simple, profound, and easily remembered.

As I walked on in my newfound faith, two things changed right away.

One, I really wanted a Bible.

Two, I had a desire to play a musical instrument.

So, a Bible. Where would I find, borrow, or purchase a Bible? I didn't wonder for long. An organization called the Gideons showed up on campus, in the form of nice gentlemen passing out pocket-sized New Testaments. And these colorful little books were...FREE! I remember standing in line and getting mine. The little green book fit right into my pocket. Top shirt pocket or back pocket—take your pick!

I never saw the Gideons again, but staying in a hotel room with my mom, I opened the nightstand drawer, and what did I find? A Gideons Bible. I thought, *These guys really get around!* I had no idea.

The Gideons International organization began distributing Bibles in 1908. Over 260,000 Gideons serve, with many more supporters around the world. The Gideons don't get paid; they pay to be part of the organization. And they've placed more than two billion Bibles and New Testaments around the world, in hotels, motels, convalescent homes, doctors' offices, shelters, prisons, and yes, military schools.

Across the years, I must have worn out twenty or thirty of these pocket Bibles, including the one in my left back pocket right now. Its corners are bent, the color faded, and the pages well-worn. It's there for me. Anywhere, anytime. Amen.

———

When I came home for the summer in 1972, I realized I needed a full-sized Bible to call my own. People at the Bible studies all had bigger Bibles. Well, not as big as the one on Mr. Swanson's table, but bigger than the pocket-sized version. Those Bibles definitely had more pages. So, time to make a purchase. I looked in the phone book and discovered where to go.

The perfect store, ladies and gentlemen: Valley Book and Bible, right there on Van Nuys Boulevard. I rode my ten-speed bike, found a place to secure it, and walked in. I couldn't believe it. Kind of like the Tardis spaceship in *Doctor Who*, it was way bigger on the inside.

Bibles. *Bibles.* No, I mean, hundreds if not thousands of Bibles! And T-shirts. And bracelets. And different kinds of books, for adults and kids. And record albums—some of them rock and roll! But that's another story.

I went to the counter and asked perhaps the dumbest and smartest question of my life: "Can I get a Bible?"

The kind man, probably a Sunday school teacher, looked at me through his glasses. He may have been thinking, *Son, we have a hundred million to choose from.*

But he said, "What kind of Bible do you want?"

"Well, what kind should I get?"

"That all depends. What translation do you like?"

"Um, the one that talks about Jesus."

The man must have known I was a new believer. Correction: baby believer.

"Do you want a New Testament?"

I was struggling. "You mean like, a new one or a used one?"

"We only sell new Bibles. You probably want both Old and New Testaments, right?"

I just didn't know *anything* about Bibles. I was trying to compare Bibles to newspapers or magazines, with a current issue (new) or an outdated issue (old). He eventually stepped in and took over. In a gentle way.

"I think you want a Bible with Old and New Testaments. Follow me."

I did get a Bible, and I was so proud of it. But there were so many pages! It was over two thousand pages—this was a *big* book! I didn't know if I'd ever finish it.

I did find the New Testament part, and was thrilled to see the words of Christ in red print. Mostly, I read in the four Gospels, and specifically hunted for the words *Jesus* or *Christ*. I read those words and felt like I was eating a meal. Having an experience. A close encounter...of the spiritual kind.

I thought, innocently, that after reading a verse (with Jesus in it), I was ready to teach it. Preach it. Proclaim it. The S as in Self was creeping back up onto the throne!

I just knew my friends and family would want to hear about the Bible and Jesus and me—the new, born-again, Jesus-loving, Christianized Rod Butler. And I was ready to tell them all about it!

You can probably feel the turbid, muddy undercurrents in that excitement. It was too early. I was so young in my faith. And they had no warning of what was coming.

An overzealous new believer, like a puppy off the leash, can do a lot of damage....

So I had a Bible. Next on the list: a musical instrument.

I'd learned to play drums at Ridgewood, but wanted something that would make musical notes, for melodies.

Somewhere in the San Fernando Valley, I found a music store, bicycled there, and looked for something inexpensive. Especially less expensive than a Bible.

At the counter, I found a recorder. A plastic recorder. Like a flute, except you blow directly into it, rather than blowing across a hole on the side. Yes, the kind little kids play in elementary school. I bought it. And learned to play it. Sort of.

When I say play it, I don't mean reading music but just following the instructions for making notes—pleasing notes—come out of the little toy instrument. Lots of shrill, overblown, and off-the-scale notes came out of that little tube, but after time, I could play a scale, from bottom to top and back down. Without ear damage to me or my mother, who probably closed her door and all the other doors between her and the recorder.

Armed with that knowledge, I made up melodies. I tried to make them worshipful melodies, if that makes sense. I thought, *If I can pray to the Lord, and he hears me; sing to the Lord and he listens; why not raise a wordless prayer, like pure melodious praise?*

I guess I figured the birds praise him. Sun, moon, and stars praise him. All of creation praises him—and none of them use words. Why can't I do the same?

So then, along with my Bible and my pocket New Testament, I had my recorder, baptized in breath and made-up melodies. I felt just wonderful.

But to those around me, my family, and during the school year, my fellow cadets, I was more odd than Rod.

To them, I was officially just one of those Jesus freaks.

*There are two worlds, in the one world we know.*
*The second world is hidden, like water in snow.*
*The first world is present, in the noise of every day.*
*The second is beyond, and shall never pass away.*

# Chapter 11
# WONDERS

There's a phrase in the New Testament: "signs and wonders."

In John's Gospel, we read:

> At Capernaum there was an official whose son was ill. When this man heard that Jesus had come from Judea to Galilee, he went to him and asked him to come down and heal his son, for he was at the point of death. So Jesus said to him, "Unless you see signs and wonders you will not believe." (John 4:46–48)

The small group of ANA cadets who had become Christians now included my buddies Greg Shannon and Dave Alwardt, and we were happy in our newfound faith. We knew that, in the sphere of life at the Academy, Jesus was alive and working among us. We didn't need signs to believe or wonders to keep us following Christ, but amazingly, these weeks were filled with signs on parade and wonders displayed.

When I say "sign," I guess I think of a stop sign or an under-construction sign. Or—if I can say it this way—God signing his name on the people and places around us. These were "autograph days," God's Son signing his name through the visible evidences of his presence. And flowing from his presence were also wonders—again, my definition—accomplishments above and beyond the normal things we were accustomed to. Take for example, Sergeant Major Ready.

At the Academy, we all kinds of teachers. Many of them were memorable, several unforgettable, and that included Sergeant Major Earl Ready.

I nicknamed him Rough and Ready, though his name was pronounced "*ray*-dee." He was a rough-looking, chisel-faced man, like a Robert De Niro maybe. Not tall, but bulldog tough, and yes, almost New York gangster material. A retired Army man, he was in charge of the armory where we learned to fire a rifle and take apart said rifle bit by bit, to clean it carefully and put it back together. Hopefully without leftover parts. Sergeant Major Ready was down there, ruling the roost, spicy, blunt, and all business.

So it was quite a surprise when, one morning in chapel, at the mandatory weekly service, he stepped up to the mic to address the audience. By audience, I mean cadets and faculty. He spoke to us openly and honestly. Without restraint.

His tone was soft, pliable. *Was he okay? Was he sick?* He began to talk about his life, admitting he was an awful person. He was visibly heartbroken. Where was Rough and Ready? What was happening here?

Now, in chapel no specific religion was ever mentioned. Colonel Atkinson's favorite saying was "A new broom sweeps clean," and that sort of thing. But Sergeant Major Ready? He broke the broom.

He told us he had repented of his sins and given his heart to Jesus Christ. He gave his full testimony and said he would be around afterward if anyone wanted to talk to him. He announced a weekly service in the chapel for any who wanted to stop by and hear more about becoming a Christian. Truly, you could hear the proverbial pin drop.

My Academy buddy Dave Alwardt recalls it vividly:

"I remember Sergeant Major Ready giving his testimony. I'd never heard anything like it before, and I was raised in the Lutheran church my grandfather had built. Later that day, after class, I looked him up, and he told me to come to his PTL (Praise the Lord) meeting. Okay, so I went, and after listening to what was said, I knew that was what I needed. I prayed but felt nothing. I wandered outside the chapel and stood near this big bush. I was praying and suddenly started crying. Wondering what was going on, I asked Sergeant Ready what was happening to me. He said it was the Holy Spirit touching my heart. That's when everything exploded! It was like, oh, okay, that makes sense, and I became so happy that I just floated around the campus for about four days. Couldn't stop telling people I got saved."

Another cadet, a sophomore, Paul Carden, was also swept into the kingdom. As Mr. Carden's son, Paul joined Masque & Wig as a great actor, but was also a cartoonist, writer, and very funny person, though serious at the first meeting. I shared my faith with Paul, and later, in the chapel, kneeling with a small group that met for prayer, he surrendered his life to Christ. Paul would go on to establish a world-wide ministry, the Center for Apologetics Research (CFAR), equipping believers to defend their faith and counteract cult organizations.

In those days at ANA, even getting a haircut became a spiritual experience. All cadets basically got the same haircut from the same barber—the only barber—Ray Bobbitt.

He was a kind man, a bit portly, with a southern accent and a hair-tonic aroma. I wasn't sure if being bald really qualified him to give us haircuts (ha ha). But then again, if every cut was the same, I guess it worked. Fortunately, we *did* walk away with our own haircut and not his, um, non-hair haircut. Anyway.

I remember sitting in the mirrored room with the white sheet spread over my body and snapped together at the neck. When I told Ray I was a new Christian, he suddenly revealed his true profession: a Sunday school teacher with (what I thought was) all knowledge of the Bible—every verse—every chapter—every book —from start to finish.

Butler, at the opposite end of that, knew a little about the Gospel of John. Period. I could find it because I had a piece of paper wedged between the pages where I was reading. But here, mummified, snapped up, and unable to grab my Gideon's New Testament, I was easy prey.

Each haircut session was transformed into a Bible Quiz-a-thon.

"Butlah," Ray would start, even before the scissors snipped, "what does it say in Exodus chapter (whatever) and verse (whatever)?" I've since heard that the answer to every Christian question can somehow be Jesus, but I didn't know that at the time.

Sulking amid the snipping, I replied, "I dunno, Ray, is it about love?" He paused, then led us into concepts and characters I'd never heard of. Words and biblical names completely foreign to me. I kept quiet, which was the best thing at the time.

Ray-Baba (as Horner and I called him) meant well, and I know his goal was to get me acquainted with God's Word. I'm grateful for that. I needed a wake-up call to the incredible breadth and depth of the Scripture, and it echoed my late-night wake-up call, "You've got a lot of work to do."

*Now the barber is a scholar; the rifleman sheds a tear.*
*Those with shrouded vision, their eyesight becomes clear.*
*Bullies and drug users, people bound now breaking free,*
*And look who's in the midst of it—whaddah ya know—it's me!*

Chapter 12

# AROUND THE WORLD

WHAT WAS GOING ON AT ANA WAS HAPPENING AROUND THE world.

Our local experience was part of a global phenomenon.

The Jesus Movement lasted from the 1970s through the 1980s. Funny that, as I've been writing this book, the movie *Jesus Revolution* was released, portraying the story through the eyes of Chuck Smith, the pastor of Calvary Chapel; Greg Laurie, a young artist; and Lonnie Frisbee, a street preacher and evangelist.

Watching the movie was a rare experience, knowing I was a small part of it all. A few moments really touched home.

Of course, back then, we high school cadets had no idea how far this kind of experience was spreading. The movement is said to have begun on the West Coast of the United States (ANA was in Carlsbad, California) and then caught fire through North America, Europe, and Central America. It was typified by people getting "saved" and becoming "Jesus people."

The buzzword "born-again" became a common term, though it dates back to Jesus' encounter with Nicodemus in John 3:1–3, when the Lord said to him, "'Truly, truly, I say to you, unless one is born again he cannot see the kingdom of God.'"

Brian Horner and his wife Jackie, who now serve the Lord in Belize, haven't been able to watch the movie yet. As we emailed back and forth, he told me about how his story tied into the big story.

> "I got saved June 15th, 1969, in the original, smaller
> Calvary Chapel, the one you see in the flick. Lonnie Frisbee
> was preaching that night and the service was packed. By the
> time he got to his altar call I was eager to do whatever it

took to get with JESUS! After I prayed the sinner's prayer, one of the hippies invited people to another room for more prayer. If there was MORE, I wanted it! Lonnie was laying hands on people and they'd start praying or singing, getting really excited. Then Lonnie came up to me, put his hand on my forehead, and prayed for me to receive the Holy Spirit. It was a bit noisy in there, people singing with passion—but it wasn't overly loud or chaotic. It was done 'decently and in order,' as Pastor Chuck always said. That night was so incredibly beautiful. It was the defining moment of my life."

These new believers, like Brian, gathered in small groups, available homes, larger communes, and often flocked to the ocean for water baptisms. The movie effectively captured the scene: crowds gathered along the rocky shoreline, awaiting their turn, as one by one new converts were submerged in the sparkling water and lifted back up —overwhelmed with joy.

I mentioned my heart being touched by *Jesus Revolution*. Two scenes especially.

When Greg Laurie is baptized. Lonnie plunges him down and Greg drifts surrealistically in a time-suspended moment, lower and lower, bubbles like stars in space...until sunlight brightens his face and pulls him upward. He reaches and breaks the surface, a new man.

And when Greg approaches Chuck Smith with an idea for a Gospel tract titled *LIVING WATER*. We see his illustrations. Chuck smiles approvingly. And then a box is delivered, packed with the colorful tracts—hundreds of them. That got me. Because I still have one of those tracts. I almost wish I'd stood up in the theater, lifting it in the air, "Hey! Look! I've still got mine!"

So many street people, beach bums, and hippies gave their lives to the Lord. Many began attending already established churches, which brought a sudden burst in attendance. But for some who had attended the church for years, these new arrivals were often met with quizzical looks and maybe just a touch of harsh judgment.

One pastor recounted this kind of interaction. A lady sided up to him, not happy with the bare-footed, wild-haired people attending *her* church. She said, "I'm glad their souls are saved, I just want the rest of them to be saved too."

The central focus at that time was Calvary Chapel of Costa Mesa, pastored by Chuck Smith. Brian I went to Calvary frequently. It was not that far from the Academy and even closer when I attended a college in Costa Mesa, which, back in the seventies, was a sleepy, cozy place with one-story buildings and neatly plotted furrows of farmland.

Pastor Chuck looked a bit like Captain Stubing on a TV show called *The Love Boat*, with his infectious smile and bright eyes but without the button-up jacket and captain's hat. Chuck, as he was often called, had a calm, inviting style, as he taught verse by verse through the entire Bible, Sunday after Sunday through the year.

Not only was Calvary a thriving, ever-expanding, God-glorifying church but a well-spring that fountained up a whole new genre of music.

The word *maranatha* was another popular term among Jesus people. With a raised hand and extended forefinger, pointing to the sky, we'd say, "Maranatha!" This comes from I Corinthians 16:22, where

Paul writes, "Our Lord, come!" In the Greek, the word is maranatha.

Chuck Smith founded Maranatha! Music in 1971. He wanted to promote the "Jesus music" written and performed by talented young hippie musicians at Calvary as well as up and down the California coast.

The early Maranatha! groups included Love Song, Children of the Day, The Way, Debby Kerner, Mustard Seed Faith, and Daniel Amos.

Jesus music became a new sensation, and as I mentioned, these were some of the rock 'n roll albums I saw at the Bible bookstore in Van Nuys.

I flipped through the names. Here I found Barry McGuire, Love Song, 2nd Chapter of Acts, and others. I loved these three artists/groups in particular and got to see them all in concert. I knew Barry McGuire's gravel-deep voice from his song on the radio, *Eve of Destruction*. Seeing Barry and 2nd Chapter live at the Church on the Way was a highlight. I can still see him, stompin' his foot, beltin' out his songs, lovin' his Lord.

Years down the road, I was working at KCBI Radio in Dallas-Fort Worth, producing/performing my Saturday morning program, *The Coconut Hut Radio Show*. I came across Barry's name and number —and gave him a call. He answered! We had a fun chat, and he recorded an intro for one of Barry's kid's songs we played frequently. I loved hearing that voice as the song ramped up. "Hey, I'm Barry McGuire, and this is my song, 'Bullfrogs n' Butterflies' on *The Coconut Hut Radio Show!*"

Brian and I saw Love Song in concert, with Chuck Girard and the band delivering a baptized Beach Boys sound. I was especially struck by the drum solo, where drummer John Mehler opened his Bible and read Psalm 150, which he "interpreted" in a mash-up/crash-up of drums and cymbals. Praising the Lord took on a new meaning!

One time at Calvary Chapel, the country-western band Daniel Amos did a mini-concert, wearing great big cowboy hats. They had amazing harmonies and unforgettable melodies. I call them the born-again Beatles, as they shape-shifted through all the musical genres of the ensuing years. Of all the Maranatha! Music groups, DA (as they call themselves) continues to produce excellent albums.

As a teenager, I was excited about this new Christian music and didn't want anything to do with my old "worldly" music. In my dorm room at ANA, I had a footlocker tightly stuffed with albums. The ones I'd been collecting for years: Monkees, Beatles, Doors, Moody Blues, Jethro Tull, Led Zeppelin, Spooky Tooth, Jefferson Airplane, Blood, Sweat & Tears, Emerson, Lake & Palmer, and Yes. Plus, movie soundtracks and a few electronic music records.

In my unbridled enthusiasm and reckless zeal, I decided to go all out for the Lord and...throw some of the albums like Frisbees against the exterior dormitory walls.

On a sunny afternoon, I watched the vinyl discs shattering against the brick, breaking away in fragments that, of course, I later cleaned up, picking bits and pieces out of the grass. I was about three or four albums into it when a buddy of mine, not a Jesus person, came up to talk to me.

It was Nelson from my Houdini days at Ridgewood. We had been good friends, but now he was beginning to think I was crazy. I'll never forget what he said. He loved those same groups, those songs, those albums—the ones I was obliterating—and said that music was part of what tied our friendship together. That and the quest for each of us to find a girlfriend.

Anyway. He asked why he would ever want to become a Christian, if it meant giving up his music and his albums. I suddenly saw how it must have looked to him. And just as I remember him walking up to rescue me from being tied to the pull-up bars at Ridgewood, I also remember him at ANA, walking away, the shards of broken records behind him on the lawn.

Further down the road, I'm glad to say Nelson and I continued our friendship. I wish I had paid more attention to the weight of Nelson's remarks. And I continue to pray for him and his family. But Nelson's response wasn't the only one like that.

Many of my friends at the Academy didn't want my friendship anymore.

*Why is this happening?* I wondered. It couldn't be because I was riding around on their shoulders, pounding on their heads with my pocket New Testament, promising to stop if they became believers, could it? (I didn't actually do that, but in a way, it was happening.)

I didn't mean to, but I now see that I was coming on too strong, probably bringing up my faith in every conversation. Pushing them to make a decision.

The last thing I wanted was to alienate anyone from Jesus or from my friendship. But I was so overcome with what had happened to me that, sadly, I lost sight of the precious value of having friends.

More on that later, but back to the journey overall.

Overall, yes, it was an amazing journey, and I did become a better person in many other ways.

Like the tide reaching reaching across the shore, new life was spreading among the cadets of Army and Navy Academy, and many cadets experienced profound life changes. Many sad hearts were transformed into glad hearts. I was one of those glad hearts, and the glad adventures were just beginning.

Dave Alwardt summed it up when he said, "It was such an incredible time and I don't think I fully appreciated that fact until much later. I do miss how things were then. No going back."

*Calvary Chapel, on Sunday morning, packed to the brim.*
*After church, as we shuffled out, I stopped, "Look, it's him."*
*He was shaking hands at the door, this gentle pastor-man,*
*I said, "Hello, Pastor Chuck," and extended my hand.*
*I thanked him sincerely, "You've helped me so much to grow,"*
*He looked at me and smiled. "Oh, praise the Lord, doncha' know."*

# Chapter 13
# LIVING WATER

IN THOSE DAYS, CHURCH WAS CHURCH. A CHURCH BUILDING. Where churchy things happen. But that concept was about to change.

One thing I liked about going to Mass was that it was always the same. And it didn't last too long. I knew when to stand, when to sit, when to kneel on the kneeling support. I didn't really have to listen to what was being said, and some of it was in Latin anyway. When Mass was over, Mutti and I left right away (she didn't know that many people) and went straight to the waiting taxicab.

The only unpredictable part was when the leader said, "Let us turn to one another and offer the sign of peace." To me, the sign of peace was when you raised two fingers into a V and said, in a hippie voice, "Peace, dude." I didn't do that, but I did always turn to Mutti and say, what she would say back to me, "Peace be with you." Pretty simple stuff.

But there was another kind of church meeting, or un-churchy meeting that happened in the Jesus Days. Christians gathered in small groups, usually formed their chairs into a circle, and held Bible studies, prayer times, or fellowship meetings (sometimes with food).

One of those meetings would turn out to change my life. But I'm getting ahead of myself.

I told you about the *LIVING WATER* tract by Greg Laurie. The coolest tract I ever received and the only one I still have. Those two words, in cartoon lettering, seemed to dance in front of an up-gushing fountain of water, the whole illustration fresh, cartoony, unforgettable. Greg Laurie would years later become a world-wide evangelist and popular radio Bible teacher. Anyway, I remember first seeing those words, and wondering what that really meant.

*Living...water? How can water be alive? And how would you ever drink it?* Like: *Come back here, water! I'm thirsty!*

Of course, I didn't know it then, but it's one of the marvelous, mysterious sayings of Jesus:

> "On the last day of the feast, the great day, Jesus stood up and cried out, "If anyone thirsts, let him come to me and drink. Whoever believes in me, as the Scripture has said, 'Out of his heart will flow rivers of living water.' Now this he said about the Spirit, whom those who believed in him were to receive..." (John 7:37–39)

A few weeks after my top-bunk prayer, I began hearing about the Holy Spirit. I knew about the phrase, "In the name of the Father, and the Son, and the Holy Spirit," so I knew about the Trinity, but hadn't thought much about the third member, the Holy Spirit. Some cadets were talking about it and how a Christian should be *filled* with the Holy Spirit.

Then Dr. Bill Bright's influence showed up again. I didn't know it, but he had put out a second tract after *The Four Spiritual Laws*. I snatched this one up, like a new book from a New York Times best selling author!

The tract, *Have You Made the Wonderful Discovery of the Spirit-Filled Life?*, had a solid blue cover with those words and a cartoon dove. I remember his point: Christians can fall into a pattern of directing their own lives. This is not what God intended. This self-directed life can be replaced by the Spirit-filled life. Each Christian can be filled (directed and empowered) by the Holy Spirit. Then Christ lives his life in and through us, by virtue of the Holy Spirit's power.

After reading this little booklet with big ideas, Dave and I were on the lookout for someone to help us to be filled with the Spirit.

Along with Brian Horner, we had been attending one of those Bible study groups in a cozy little motel at Tamarack Beach, a short walk along the coastline from the Academy. This was my first experience with such a group and I vividly remember the experience of being there.

Dressed in our uniforms, we left the Army Navy campus and took the sidewalk that looked across to the beach and the ocean. Soon a motel came into view, white-walled and low-roofed. A few palm trees were likely there to greet us. We turned and walked into the lobby.

The room was full of hippies! Long hair, beards, T-shirts, jeans, bead-necklaces, and of course, Bibles. And I think they were all smiling! Just like in the movie.

Well, you have to understand that, in previous visits to church, marching in formation, it wasn't unusual to hear somebody call out to us, "Hey, jarheads!" That was slang for Marines, likely stationed at Camp Pendleton in Oceanside. But it was hailed out to cadets too.

I was ready for people in the room to stare at us, thinking "jarheads," but they didn't. I thought they would look at our name-plates and say, "So you're, let's see, BUTLER." "And you must be, um, is it, ALWARDT?" But they didn't do that. In fact, they seemed to look past our haircuts and uniforms.

Boldly, for me, I offered a handshake—but these people were huggers! Nobody hugged at St. Cyril's. I only hugged Mutti, really, ever. They treated us like lifelong friends. What was going on?

True to form, they had arranged folding chairs in a tight circle. Weird! No pews, no robes, no pulpit. Definitely no saxophones. Was this church, actually?

We found empty chairs and sat down. And then stood back up and —gulp—held hands. Okay. Wait. I really didn't hold hands—not with guys—and not at church. Wasn't that an unspoken law? Don't talk to strangers, don't take candy from strangers, don't hold hands with strangers? At least I was holding hands with Dave and a stranger. But even that felt funny.

Then a few different people prayed, but not memorized prayers. Casual prayers, talking to the Lord like talking to a friend, sometimes mentioning people they were concerned about.

Then we opened our Bibles. In those days I still had the little green New Testament, so I opened that, though it felt like opening a baby Bible or something.

The leader presided over the study, but people were free to talk about what the verses meant to them. I was beginning to like this! We came back to the meeting several times. And about the second or third time—it happened.

We arrived a little late, and something different was going on.

It looked like a huddle in football—you know, when the guys are tightly gathered around, setting up the play. The difference was this: there was one person in the middle. And all the people's hands were on this person's head and shoulders.

This was as far away from St. Cyril's as anyone could ever get. I felt a little funny about it, but I felt at home too. My eyes were riveted on the huddle, because the leader, a heavyset hippie with a big beard, someone I'd not seen before, was praying, "Lord, bless my brother, bless him, bless him real good."

Others were praying too. Their voices were united. Not in unison but in fervor. In compassion. Then there was a breakthrough moment, and I guess the brother in need was blessed or encouraged, because the huddle broke up and we got ready for Bible study. I did not know—Dave did not know—that the next huddle would be for us.

*They gathered together in the upper room,*
*Their souls united, their hearts in tune.*
*Then, flames of fire, and a great rushing wind!*
*As God, his Holy Spirit, he did powerfully send.*

Chapter 14

# THE NEXT HUDDLE

Horner never told me that when I became a Christian there would be dessert.

You can laugh, but it's very significant. Food is part of Christianity. Part of the biblical narrative.

In the Old Testament, milk and honey, barley bread, grapes and peaches, and maybe it shouldn't be mentioned, but, okay...apples.

New Testament: The feeding of the five thousand. The Last Supper. Breakfast on the beach with Jesus. And, in heaven, the Marriage Supper of the Lamb. And so on.

That's why—and I think it made good sense—there was dessert at the Bible study in the lobby of the little motel at Tamarack Beach.

When the meeting broke up, we moved to a time of fellowship. Again, the opposite of me and Mutti scurrying for the cab. These people loved just being together.

I heard laughter, talking, and Scripture being discussed. I felt a general warmth about everything. For some reason, a song by The Turtles comes to mind, the chorus being, "So happy together."

And again, the fact that we three "jarheads," BUTLER, HORNER, and ALWARDT, were there in GI Joe clothing didn't matter at all. I've come to know this, now, as the wonder of the body of Christ, God's people, united, yet diversified, gathering together, and Jesus promising to be in the midst of them: "For where two or three are gathered in my name, there I am among them" (Matthew 18:20).

Part of the fellowship time was food-o-ship time. (Just made that up.) I mean, a small card table was topped with paper plates, Styrofoam cups for coffee or tea, and a store-bought pie, fresh out of the box, next to plastic forks and napkins. Heaven for high school cadets. Dave and I were munching down fork-fulls of pie when I pointed out the lady in charge of refreshments. The lady slicing the pie. The lady with a big smile.

I spoke quietly to Dave.

"Dave, look at the pie lady. That smile. Maybe she knows about the Holy Spirit." Dave agreed, and I was sent on a mission. Thanks, Dave. I meandered up to the pie lady and asked, very casually, very quietly, "Ma'am, I was wondering...if you knew anything about...being filled with the Holy Spirit?"

There was a pause. Then she smiled more than ever. In a full voice she said, "Oh, yes! You can be filled with the Holy Spirit RIGHT NOW!" Before I could interrupt—"Everybody! This young man is ready to be filled with the Holy Spirit!" Suddenly Dave was next to me, and there we were in the huddle with Horner and the bearded brother, and the brethren surrounding us.

Bearded brother said he was going to pray for us to be filled with Spirit of God. I guessed he knew about the Bill Bright tract. After that happens, he said, we might receive a heavenly language. Immediately I was worried. My thoughts were racing. *What was it? How would I know it? Or say it?* I confess, I may have suddenly longed for the taxicab at St. Cyril's.

And then Dave began to whisper, like a trickling stream of words, just barely there. I thought, *Dave! No! Don't leave me behind!*

There was a struggle inside me. A battle really. Dave's spiritual language was strengthening. But I was still left out and frustrated— trying to catch something outside my grasp. The bearded brother was right there, gently encouraging me. So. I stepped out. To the edge of the diving board. To the border of the map. Into the unknown.

*Did I trust God? Yes, I did. Would he lead me astray? No, he never would. Does he love me, right here, right now? Yes and yes and YES.*

*So...*

By now the whole group had surrounded us and was praying. I don't know, it was kind of like people in the grandstands cheering us on, "You can do this. You can do this!"

So I did it. I whispered what came to me: foreign—maybe otherworldly—words. I whispered those words. Words I'd never spoken. Words I wasn't making up, like when I was being a funny character. What I hoped were...words from heaven.

Nobody laughed. Nobody applauded, but hey, apparently, I wasn't a failure.

And so, quietly, I heard myself speaking a language I had never learned.

Something very encouraging happened then—a kind of rejoicing from the Christians around us. Yet, it wasn't really directed at us—it seemed to be lifted up, to the roof, or the sky beyond, or the heavenly realm beyond that.

I thought of the blue tract. And the white cartoon dove. And the other tract, with the words *LIVING WATER*. I was so happy. I had received the Holy Spirit.

Maybe it was the best inhale and the most refreshing exhale...of my lifetime.

All was well. Throughout the universe, across the galaxy, down on earth, and in the motel, with a collection of hippies, locals, and cadets, all was well.

Walking back to the Academy, serenaded by surf sounds and canopied by the silent majesty of stars, I felt like a different person.

The terrestrial had encountered the celestial.

Or, the celestial had embraced the thankful terrestrial. Or both.

It was as if I'd been given a gift I did not deserve.

It was like being at home in the King's palace when I wasn't born of royal lineage. I had a present when it wasn't my birthday; I received a treasure I could never, ever afford.

I thought of priests, or monks, who gave up marriage and family life, a secular career, other pleasantries, to live completely in God's service. It cost them something.

But here I was, slipping into my heavenly language now and then, a caretaker of a gift beyond time and space. There was a supernatural dynamic to my life now. Though I still couldn't explain it, or really comprehend it.

I'm thinking here of the *Lord of the Rings* movies, the first movie, with the wizard Gandalf saying to Frodo Baggins, regarding the ring of mighty power the little Hobbit possesses, "Keep it secret, keep it safe." And so I have, from that day to this.

I did a lot of praising that night, even while brushing my teeth. I climbed into my bed on the top bunk, exhilarated. It sounds strange maybe, but I felt so in love with Jesus. He was alive inside me, and now his Spirit, like a river, flowed out from me.

Here I was, loving this person I couldn't see or touch or hug. But he was present. Real. And he loved me too.

I wonder if my thoughts that night could have echoed the elegant words of Saint Augustine of Hippo, who lived from 354 to 430, when he wrote:

"But what do I love when I love you? Not the beauty of any body or the rhythm of time in its movement; not the radiance of light, so dear to our eyes; not the sweet melodies in the world of manifold sounds; not the perfume of flowers, ointments and spices; not manna and not honey; not the limbs so delightful to the body's embrace; it is none of these things that I love when I love my God.

And yet when I love my God I do indeed love a light and a sound and a perfume and a food and an embrace—a light and sound and perfume and food and embrace in my inward self. There my soul is flooded with a radiance which no space can contain; there a music sounds which time never bears away; there I smell a perfume which no wind disperses; there I taste a food that no surfeit embitters; there is an embrace which no satiety severs. It is this that I love when I love my God." (Confessions 10.6.8)

*The ways of God can be puzzling, yes, even strange,*
*Think of the tadpole or the caterpillar's great change.*
*Think of the wind, you can't grasp—you only hear it,*
*So mysterious and wise are the ways of the Spirit.*

# PART TWO
## After

Chapter 15

# BACK TO SHERMAN OAKS

HOME FROM MY JUNIOR YEAR AT ANA, I WAS REUNITED WITH the sights and sounds of my hometown: Sherman Oaks.

I rode my 10-speed down the winding streets under the palm trees, all the way to the book and Bible store to buy a record album, sealed in clear plastic.

In my room, I unwrapped the record, opened the old record player, and dropped the needle to the vinyl groove. Christian rock 'n roll.

Around me were my things from childhood, on the shelves, in the places where they'd been for so many years. It felt a bit strange, since I'd grown up, but the room hadn't changed at all. Trumpet lamp, models, everything. And most of it covered in a thin layer of dust.

There would be Friday night outings to Bullock's Fashion Square, and a meal at the Jolly Roger Restaurant with my mom. Swimming at Mutti's pool. Getting together with Caren, Chris, and Jenny and the Encino gang. Going to Mark and Bonnie's house. The whole summer spread out before me, and at the heart of it: one very special thing I'd been looking forward to.

Telling each of them about my born-again experience. I'd planned it out, and I was ready.

I'd begin with meeting Brian Horner, and repeat pretty much what he told me, explain how I prayed the prayer—twice—and then the next day went around walking on air. They'd love that!

Never did I reflect back on Nelson and the broken albums. Or other friends who were confused, almost disappointed in who I'd become.

But these were family and friends—this was home! They'd see the change in me, and, I was 99 percent sure, they would want to meet Jesus too.

Of course, I wouldn't talk about the Holy Spirit or any of those things—those might be too unusual, but I had what they called my "testimony" all worked out, and I knew who I would tell first.

I arrived at Mutti's house, ready to swim and have a Mutti meal. She would make me a cold glass of Hawaiian Punch with a plastic stir-stick that sported a little whistle on the end.

I can picture us, sitting in her living room, talking, explaining my new life. But as I spoke—with growing uneasiness—I watched confusion spread over her face.

"I'm a Christian now, Mutti, a born-again Christian."

"Vat do you mean, my dear? You have always been a Christian."

"Jesus Christ is in my heart now, Mutti, right now."

"Ya, but Christ comes every time you take ze sacrament."

"I know, but this is different—it's not a religion, it's a relationship."

"Vat do you mean, exuctly?"

Even with English being Mutti's third language, I had never had a difficult conversation with her. This one was deeply difficult. I felt a kind of wedge coming between us.

After a long conversation, she was mildly satisfied but very disappointed that I would no longer be going to St. Cyril's with her. I would miss those times, too.

But I thought Mutti would be glad and would want the closer relationship with Jesus I had. But I should have realized what was going on from her point of view.

I was laying aside the religion that was as special to her as my new faith was to me. She took it with grace and wisdom and, I suppose, added it to the knowledge of her other two grandsons, Rudy and Gary, not going to church at all.

This was the first of several disconnects in the San Fernando Valley, my home.

I don't like sharing these stories. But they belong to the big picture.

Mark and Bonnie attended Catholic Church, but not as regularly as Mutti. They listened to my story, and things went on, continuing as usual, but now there was a part of me they didn't understand. I suppose it was like a bruised place in a banana, if that's not too weird of an illustration. I was still Roddy, still loved Laurel and Hardy, Bugs Bunny, and sci-fi movies, but a part of me was foreign to them. I never meant for that to happen. I never saw it coming.

My Encino friends had a similar response. Again, an invisible wedge worked its way into longstanding relationships. I didn't know what to do about it. I couldn't leave my newfound faith, but I wanted somehow to stitch together these pieces that were tearing apart. So with a bit of a spiritual limp, I kept walking forward.

My mom, who sort of just rolled with things, seemed like she might be interested in the faith I had found. She hadn't gone to Mass in years but still prayed to the saints when she lost a bracelet or had trouble with the vacuum cleaner.

Later that summer, we both kneeled at the foot of her rollaway bed, and she prayed to receive Jesus Christ as her Savior. This began another journey, both wonderful and funny, introducing her to a non-Catholic church. Because, by this time, I knew I couldn't go back to the Catholic way.

But where would I go? I didn't know what existed outside the Catholic way. I may have heard the word Baptist or Presbyterian, but that was it.

I'd visited that church in Carlsbad, the one with the saxophone pastor, but I didn't know what kind of church that was, or if there were others like it. I'd visited Chuck Smith's church, and I would have loved to go there, but on a bike, it would have taken days. So to find a new church, here in the Valley, what did I do?

Once again, I got out the phone book. It was kind of like the paper internet of those days. You remember it, right? The big, thick, flimsy book with a hundred million phone numbers and addresses. The only illustrations were ads that people paid for, to make their businesses stand out. Yet I, for one, always skipped over them to get to more phone numbers.

It opened with a *THUMP!* I flipped page after page to get to the church section and started alphabetically, scanning through everything that started with A.

Imagine running your finger along an endless list of church names, but of course no description of any kind. It's so different now, with easy-to-find online sites, blogs, videos...all kinds of ways to see what a church is like. So you know what to expect.

But, in 1972, with a quick prayer, I let my finger drift down the page, line by line, until I stopped at this heading: Assembly of God.

I'd never heard of it before. There were several churches under that title.

Then a certain name caught my eye. Calvary Chapel. Yes! Calvary Chapel...of Reseda. Maybe this was another Calvary, with another Chuck Smith! Yes and *yes!* Jesus music, Jesus people, Jesus teaching. Let's GO!

I unfolded a map. It would be about an hour's bike ride on my 10-speed.

I put on my jeans and a fresh T-shirt, and rode down blocks and blocks of sidewalks, through neighborhoods and busy streets, finally arriving at a little building with a highly sloped roof and a few stained glass windows. Calvary Chapel of Reseda. It kind of looked like a small ski lodge, with only a few cars in the parking lot. I didn't see any people. Well, okay, maybe it was a smaller version of Calvary. Okay.

I stowed the bike, got my full-sized Bible, and walked toward it.

Two men in suits and ties opened the front doors and shook my hand. Inside were other people with suits and ties and ladies with long dresses, looking at this T-shirt-wearing teenager with wind-swept (if not exploded) hair looking back at them. It's possible that I smelled like an hour's ride on a 10-speed bike. In the summer.

I looked around.

There were no folding chairs. No hippies. And probably no pie.

Had I come to the wrong place?

*Father Abraham went out, not knowing where he was going,*
*Christians follow the Spirit-wind, not knowing where it's blowing.*
*The disciples faced a monstrous storm, gasp-gulping, terrified!*
*Jesus spoke just a word and brought them safely to the other side.*

# Chapter 16

# HYMNS AND HAIRDOS

Piano on the left, organ on the right. No long hair. No guitars. No drums.

Suits and ties. Long flat pews—an aisle down the center, leading to a wooden pulpit, saxophone-less, I'm sure. That was the church I was sitting in.

I was pretty sure they didn't know about Barry McGuire or the 2nd Chapter of Acts. I didn't see too many other teenagers and hardly any children.

The pastor was very smiley, so that was a good sign. He was older, and other people were much older. They began to sing. And they sang very, very slowly.

The songs (hymns) had an old-fashioned sound, which everybody seemed to like, because they all sang along.

I found a book called a hymnal, which was pretending to be a Bible until you opened it and—surprise!—it had pages and pages of sheet music. Which I couldn't read. The words were sandwiched in among the notes, and each line of lyrics had a number. It was very confusing. But everyone seemed to love it.

Looking around, taking it all in, I made my decision. This is not for me. I'm young; they're old. I'm T-shirt; they're suits and ties. I'm fast music with drums; they're slow music with organ. Done. Back to the phone book. When the service was dismissed I was ready to make the journey home on the bike.

I was heading inconspicuously for the back door when Grandad stopped me. Grandad Harrel.

At the time I didn't know he was the father of Jonathan Harrel, the pastor. But he was a rugged-looking man, probably in his seventies, and he went out of his way to shake my hand. Had a good firm grip and a sincere smile. He asked my name and wanted to know about me. He said he was happy that I had visited and hoped I'd return.

Several other people caught me before I made it to the door. Pastor Harrel and his wife, Norma, a smiling person with a tall blonde bouffant hairdo, personally greeted me.

I had been thoroughly welcomed when I got back to the bike.

As I pedaled along the sidewalks, I got to thinking. The people were so friendly. They seemed to like me. I dunno. I might go back again. And take my mom. And her car.

My mother drove a big Lincoln Continental, which was about the size of a continent. Hence the name. I think.

And my mother herself, Marguerite Koppl Butler, though a skinny little lady, had a large, vibrant personality. She talked incessantly. She was often impatient with herself, or even mean to herself. "Oh, Maggie! Where'd you put that necklace? I need it!" "Stupid! What have I done?" "It's got to be here, *somewhere*!"

She would come to me and ask for prayers to Saint Anthony. According to the Catholic Church, St. Anthony was the patron saint of lost and stolen articles.

I'd gently defer the prayer to Jesus, who was the Savior of lost and stolen people. We'd kneel together, I'd start the prayer—and she would interrupt—reminding me to pray for the necklace, or, like I said, the vacuum cleaner. When I asked her to go to Calvary Chapel of Reseda with me, to my surprise, she agreed.

She dressed up nicely and spoke gracefully to people, who were charmed by her German-type accent. Unfortunately for my mom, her singing was the same thing as her talking, only louder. And though she listened to music regularly, she herself did not have the gift of song. As I said, it was just louder talking, with subtle pitch-changes.

So whereas Mutti had her falsetto voice in church, my mom sounded a bit like William Shatner from *Star Trek*, narrating the hymn rather than singing it.

But that was okay. She felt good there. She felt that she belonged. Which is also why I continued to attend that church for several years. It was the way they treated me. Even that time when I dumped over a whole wheelbarrow full of dirt.

I knew it was a mistake to attend the Saturday men's workday. They were building and doing man-type stuff, and probably Grandad made sure I was part of the, uh, fun.

He didn't know I had grown up without a dad and had no knowledge of hammering, screwdriving, or pushing a wheelbarrow. So when I took my turn at the wheelbarrow, I tried to be brave and pitch in, like a man.

But as you can imagine, I became the comic relief.

And why they had to have a narrow, thrown-together, scrap-wood bridge across this large dug-out area, I'll never know. I'd say it was a prank, but they weren't pranking people.

I made it almost halfway across. Then I felt the heavy barrow leaning. I tried to correct it. The more I adjusted, the more it tipped, turned, and finally wrenched free, while I watched it tumble and hit the ground with a *THUDD!*

The thing is, nobody laughed. Nobody sighed, as did the cadets at Ridgewood watching me strike out, or the cadets at ANA observing my failed basketball layups.

These people all gathered in and we got it cleaned up.

That did something to me. I was, shall we say, edified, built up, instead of being shot down and belittled. *These were the people of God,* I thought. *They're the body of Christ. They jumped in and helped me and made me want to get back in the game.*

I understood something. Something new.

Church is not just a place to go on Sunday. It's a group of people you care about, and who care about you.

I'd been hearing the terms, "church home," or "home church," and I could see there was something to it. I had my home on Valley Vista, but this was another kind of home.

This was Christ, in action, using his "homies," his body (of believers) to do his work. But there was another thing. Well, another person. Who had somehow become important to me. Though I'd only known him a few months.

Grandad Harrel.

My grandfather, on my mother's side, passed away when I was two or three. So I never really had a grandfather-person in my life. Here was Grandad, never a replacement for a bloodline grandfather, but God's gift, stepping into that kind of a role—for a season—to enrich my life. Then, and for years to come.

And, thinking about it now, I have to thank his son, Pastor Jonathan Harrel, for serving as a signpost that sent my life into a new and fresh direction. And to think I criticized his church for the songs being too slow. He was used by the Holy Spirit. Powerfully. Just sitting there in his chair at his desk, talking to me.

The pastor's office is better than the principal's office, and a lot better than the Lieutenant's office. I was sitting in Pastor Harrel's office, just talking about where I might be headed, what kind of career I might pursue. He asked what kind of things I enjoyed doing.

I told him I liked to write but didn't see that as a career. (Okay, I now write as my career.) I said I loved being funny, but being a full-time comedian? Nah. (I'm definitely a part-time comedian. Have been one for over forty years.)

I could draw but didn't want to be an artist. Or an art teacher. (True.)

He asked, "Have you ever thought about Bible college?" It was like asking, have you ever thought about becoming President or leading an army? Or colonizing Mars?

I confessed it had never crossed my mind. But—I had to add—I'd always wanted to read through the whole Bible, rather than dropping out somewhere in Leviticus or Deuteronomy.

He told me about Southern California College (SCC) in Costa Mesa, an Assemblies of God college that offered degrees in ministry and other subjects as well. He said it was accredited, which meant it provided a valid degree like any other college or university. He encouraged me to at least check it out.

So I did.

*Why do I judge what I think is best?*
*Why do I fail when sent a new test?*
*I see a wall when it's really a crest,*
*Only through providence am I rescued,*
*And then blessed!*

# Chapter 17
# PREACHERS AND PUPPETS

I FOUND LOTS OF FRIENDS IN COLLEGE—SOME OF THEM human, some of them fabric and foam.

After graduating from Army and Navy Academy in 1973, I went to Pepperdine University in Malibu and roomed with Brian Horner. That was fun!

After a year at Pep, I transferred to California State University at Northridge, (CSUN), definitely the biggest university I'd ever seen. I had a 1964 Ford Falcon Futura in those days, and I needed it to drive from class to class. The old car served me well. Until the drive-shaft fell out on the freeway. Nobody was hurt, but there was no future for the Futura.

About this time, during my CSUN years, Pastor Harrel suggested Southern California College. I remember driving up to the campus. And once again, I judged the value of a place based on how it appeared at first glance.

*This is a college?*

It had featureless, old-fashioned buildings. There were several Quonset hut structures, you know, the big, elongated steel storage facilities, with rounded, ribbed-metal roofs. They looked like huge, dented tin cans. Like the barracks from *Gomer Pyle, U.S.M.C.* on TV.

A multi-storied dormitory tried to stand proud, but it looked kind of run-down, rather old and tired. Compared to CSUN, this looked like Swanson's Ranch School without the Ranch and the Swansons. But I met with people, got a tour of the grounds, and, well, I had a good feeling about going there.

I signed up and there I was...in dormitory life again.

Nobody wore uniforms, that was good. Best of all, there were girls there. I hadn't seen girls in class from junior high through high school. We had girls at Pepperdine and CSUN, but the classrooms at SCC were much smaller and I guess, the girls were sitting closer. Or maybe it was because I had started wearing glasses.

Sitting in a desk for an eight o'clock class, in my jeans and T-shirt, I looked around me. Girls, all dressed up and looking nice. Guys in real shirts and nicer jeans. Mostly.

I decided right then and there that I needed to dress like a college guy instead of a little kid. And—very important—I decided I should start doing my hair. Somehow. My cowlicks were like metal springs, and the overall look of my hair was like...like...like a patch of weeds in a hurricane. Or a cowlick convention. Or a lesser super-hero whose power is exploding hair. It would require a strong spray. Or liquid nails. No—concrete. Anyway.

The food was good, much better than military school. And they had a nice older couple on campus, who, for a small fee, would do our laundry each week and have it ready, folded, and wrapped in clear plastic. It was a good place to be.

I made friends, but this was, in general, a very different crowd of people.

Here's Butler's Breakdown:

PKs: Pastor's kids.
MKs: Missionary's kids.
SFs: Sports freaks.
BBs: Bible brains.

And:

EEs: Everybody else.

I fit into the last group. That group included Jesus people, I guess, but there were not that many of us represented there.

Being an Assembly of God school, it carried a Pentecostal or charismatic tradition, which included practices such as raising hands in worship, believing that prophecy was for today, and speaking in a heavenly language. The more common term is speaking in tongues, but I love saying "heavenly language" as Pastor Jack Hayford would say it.

Now even though those practices were givens, it didn't mean those things happened all that much. I adjusted to that, but there was a prevalent attitude, like a hidden monster I hadn't faced before. It was this: Many students grew up in pastor's and missionary's homes and had known the Lord or heard about him all of their lives. In fact, they had almost heard *too much* about the Lord.

I mean, with parents immersed in full-time ministry, these kids grew up more in the church building than in their own homes. Many of them gave up routine lives and activities to be active on the mission field, many times in unfamiliar surroundings. This led some to apathy, or worse, a jaded attitude—making them more likely to mock spiritual people and ride the outer rails of commitment to Christ and biblical ways of life.

They could imitate preachers the way I imitated Laurel and Hardy. Well, with more exaggeration. Really, it was straightforward mockery. Or for some, just having fun.

Deep down, I think they churned with buried anger, neglect, and despondency. In some cases, attending SCC helped them climb out of the pit.

To be fair, several of these PKs and MKs went on to serve the Lord, as their parents did, with hard work and sincerity.

I'm not here to judge them; I brought plenty of my own baggage too.

Secretly, I held an exaggerated kind of agenda. I yearned to become a dynamic, brilliant, and powerful Bible teacher. A power-pastor.

I loved the teaching of Pastor Jack Hayford at the Church on the Way, and then, at SCC, the more casual but still dynamic preaching of Gayle Erwin and Dick Foth.

I saw myself as a potential Super-teacher, with suit and cape, and was heading that way, unhindered.

Until, under Gayle Erwin's teaching in several of my classes, I discovered the importance of being a servant-leader, investing in people, and in that way expanding the kingdom of God. Teaching the Bible was still a goal, but caring for people became the other half that would form a complete whole.

Something else happened at the little college in Costa Mesa.

A small thing that released a huge, lifelong thing. I should say, an event orchestrated by the Holy Spirit. For though I may not have been as amazed with the Spirit as I had been some years earlier, he was still very much with me, and I was—no thanks to my bumbling and blundering—living the Spirit-directed life.

Back to the "small thing."

It started out as a typical morning chapel service. The church-like building was full of students and teachers.

A student, Kevin O'Neil, began preaching from the pulpit. He got a few sentences into it; then he stopped. Something distracted him, and he ducked down behind the pulpit.

Two or three moments passed.

Instead of coming back up, a floppy puppet came up. The puppet began to sing from the musical *Fiddler on the Roof.*

In a thin, nasal voice, but staying on key, "Do you love meeeee?" Then another puppet popped up, while the first one stayed in place.

This time, a puppety girl voice sang back. It was, of course, Kevin doing both voices, and you could tell it was him. But who cared? We couldn't stop watching this preacher from another planet. "Yes, I love youuuuuuuu," sang the puppet. There was laughter. And silence.

Many people were awe-struck.

I was puppet-struck.

Kevin went on to finish the song and wrap up a message about loving one another. I sat there. *I could do that,* I thought. *I know I could.* I had to find Kevin and talk to him.

We became friends, and I picked up the knack for puppetry pretty quickly. I had already been doing cartoon voices, and I was good at drama, being silly my whole life. Even graduating from ANA as the president of Masque & Wig, ahem, thank you, thank you. I had been *prepared.*

I bought two of the same kind of puppets, rather Muppety-looking puppets, at Bullock's Fashion Square when I was at home, doing the Friday night outing with my mom.

First, I found a brown dog with floppy ears. Named him Freemont.

Digging deeper in the pile, I pulled out a red cow with floppy fabric horns, to be named Torkie the Red Cow. Next, a spider with dangling legs who got a New York gangster-type voice and became Pete Dah Spidah. Finally, a ball of fluff with funny eyes...the Flump.

Kevin taught me well, and we were ready for our first performance together. But I didn't expect the location. Never would have in a million years.

The oncology ward at CHOC, the Children's Hospital of Orange County.

*Sometimes we are summoned off to go,*
*Where people live at their all-time low.*
*And here in a sad and sorrowed place,*
*God will radiate his holy, hallowed face.*

# Chapter 18

# PUPPETS ON PURPOSE

Kevin knew what to do. He'd done it before, several times.

We had to wash up with disinfectant soap and then slip hospital gowns over our clothes. Then, with a duffle bag stuffed with puppets and a cardboard screen, we followed the nurse into the cancer ward.

Even being scrubbed up, I wasn't prepared for that first time. The quietness. The stillness. A feeling of emptiness in the hallways, even with people walking by. I wondered if silly, funny-voiced puppets should even be there. And then we entered our first room.

I remember crouching down behind the screen—really a dressmaker's cutting board that folded up for carrying—then taking a breath and diving into the skit. I was glad it was me and Kevin, and not just me.

There wasn't much laughter as we went from room to room, but there was a sense of doing good. I believe we were bringing God's presence, through floppy hand puppets, into difficult situations.

A smile, even a quiet laugh or a giggle, felt like unearthing a nugget of gold. We *were* making a difference. It just had to be measured in a different way. One way: they asked us back.

As we continued to visit for a year or so, I imagine the young patients could hear the puppet voices down the hall and knew what was coming. It must have been a treat, maybe something like the trained dogs that come to visit hospitals from time to time, bringing a touch of warmth and happiness.

I began to realize something.

Puppets could go places people couldn't always go. They could preach, but softly, bringing gentle messages through antics and shenanigans. Kevin and I didn't mention the name of Jesus in our hospital visits, but I feel like his Spirit still slipped through. In fact, I know the Holy Spirit was there. Because...it's a small world, after all.

One of our skits involved two puppets trying to get along with each other, a theme not far afield from Kevin's pulpit/puppet show in chapel.

When the little creatures got their act together, Kevin and I, maybe not the best vocalists, sang the song from the Disneyland attraction, "It's a Small World (After All)."

A month later we received an invitation to attend a funeral. One of the little girls, Heather, had passed away. We remembered her and her mother. We accepted, of course, and wearing suits and ties, we sat in the pew at the funeral home, waiting for the service to start.

It was already an emotional moment. But then, as part of the organ prelude, we heard a familiar melody line. The melody you know as soon as you hear it: "It's a Small World (After All)." Even being played on a soft organ, without any singing, it stood out from the hymns before and after it. And it must have stood out to Heather and her family. So they, rather unconventionally, added it to the prelude. To this day it moves me deeply.

There was something about the impact of this lower form of drama, this puppeteering. It might have been the first time I thought of the phrase, "puppet ministry."

A few weeks later, in the school cafeteria, I was handed my lunch plate by Linnie, a student worker. I knew her a little bit, as we were both part of the cafeteria crew. She had the easy job of working the line. When I came to work, I reported to the deep metal sinks to scrub the big ol' pots and pans. Wearing those heavy rubber gloves. With the super hot water, steaming up my glasses. Anyway, back to the lunch line. I took the plate with the hamburger on it and was ready to move my tray down the line.

"Are you the guy who does puppets with Kevin?" she asked.

I said I was.

"I'm part of a children's television show, and we need puppeteers."

"Well, I've only been doing puppets for a couple of months. I doubt I'm good enough."

"No, I've seen you, and you're better than some of the puppeteers we have."

That seemed to be good news and bad news together, ha ha. But sure enough, Linnie gave me the address of Trinity Broadcasting Network (TBN) in Santa Ana, not that far from Costa Mesa, and soon after I was there.

I could easily squeeze in a testimony here. *God changed my life in the cafeteria lunch-line.* Or, *Hamburger from heaven.* He *does* work in mysterious ways. Mysterious and delightful.

I was taken to a sound stage with one main set and three large video cameras ready to roll into position. The setting was park-like, with a large tree, and on a picket fence was painted the word BACKYARD.

I met the producer and creator of the show, JoAn Summers. She and her husband Bob, were pastors in Texas, but they came out once a month to shoot four episodes. In two days.

JoAn had a real heart for children, which was the genius and the genesis of the TV show. The story goes like this...

Years before, in Orange County, California, JoAn had a good number of children attending her summer Bible clubs. Many of the gatherings were in apartment complexes where kids had no back-yard. But they wanted one. The perceptive Mrs. Summers took note of that.

The Summers' friend, Paul Crouch, soon-to-be head of TBN, saw the impact of her ministry and said, "Someday, when I have my own TV station, I want you to bring this type of program to children."

Paul Crouch did get his own TV station, and Miss Jo, as she would be called in the show, got the green light and got busy. Miss Jo recalls,

"We built a set, a backyard with all the things I knew the kids enjoyed: a swing hanging from a tree; Susie, a ventriloquist with her puppet Sidney; a big dog named Barker; plus two other puppets— Needeep, a frog in a well; and Milton, a squirrel in a tree.

I felt the cast was complete, but Linnie, who played Milton, told me about Rod and his gifts as a puppeteer. I gave her the go-ahead, and she invited him to the set. I was so busy I had no time to sit down with him. However, I covertly watched as he improvised with a puppet. Then and there I decided to write another character into the show for Rod."

Backing up the story, now from my point of view.

I stood there on the set, ready for an audition or a conversation, but they were getting ready to shoot a scene, so I was asked to wait. Not a problem. I loved watching the show being taped.

One hour led to another, and I poked around, finding a Muppet-style puppet. I'd been wanting to try one of these out, so I had some quiet fun, watching the the puppet's movement in a window's reflection. I couldn't believe it. Playing with a professional puppet in a professional TV studio.

Then the cameras shut down. Hot lights went cold. Miss Jo and the cast had finished the day's shoot. People pushed the set walls away, and cast members said good-bye.

I wondered about the audition. Had she forgotten? Should I mention it? She smiled, and in her southern accent, said she would be in touch with me. I thanked her, kind of quizzically, and left the building, got into the Ford Falcon Futura and drove back to SCC.

Miss Jo says, "After returning to Texas, I wrote Rod a letter inviting him to join the *Backyard* cast. He was there for the next taping and won all our hearts immediately with his wonderful sense of humor and creativity."

Again, backing up, and from my point of view, some time passed after my visit to TBN. Then one day a letter with BACKYARD on the envelope arrived in my school mailbox. Miss Jo asked if I would be interested in playing Rubinstein Rabbit, who would have a British accent and come out of a tree to play a (rabbit-sized) grand piano.

Stuffed into the envelope was a TV script on crinkly onionskin paper. I unfolded the script noisily. Flipped through it. There was RUBINSTEIN RABBIT, his name, and his lines.

Was this really happening? Lord, I didn't know this would happen. I said yes to you, but I didn't know what was in store. This is wonderful—no, so much *more* than wonderful!

Jeremiah 29:11 unfolded before my eyes: "For I know the plans I have for you, declares the LORD, plans for welfare and not for evil, to give you a future and a hope." The Good News Translation (GNT) says, "...the future you hope for."

I had a bright future. Under a tree, with a toy piano, in a corner of the *Backyard*.

I say, old chap, time to brush up on my English accent, indeed!

> *God uses raindrops, thunderclouds, and storms,*
> *Through tiny molecules his miracles he performs.*
> *His timing is impeccable, his promises secure,*
> *His loving ways resilient and precious and pure.*

# Chapter 19
# RACHMANINOFF'S RABBIT

THANKFULLY, *Star Wars.*

The first *Star Wars* movie, *Episode 4: A New Hope* had released, and I saw it after standing in a long line at the famous Chinese Theater in Hollywood. So back at SCC, as I studied the *Backyard* script, I kept the golden robot, C3PO, centered in my mind.

The scene where C3PO says, "Well, I'm not going that way. It's much too rocky," became my starting place for Ruben. Thank you, Anthony Daniels, and your proper British tone. The day arrived, and I drove out to TBN, script in hand.

The rabbit puppet was very nicely made. I wiggled my thumb and tall finger into the paws and my index finger into the head. Ruben looked at me. I looked at Ruben. And thus became our shared existence in the world of the *Backyard*.

Miss Jo and I walked over to the big fabric-and-wood tree, and I realized what my position in this life would be. Lying on my stomach, inside and behind the tree, with my hand ready at the back of the little door.

Near the door, I had my script taped to a wooden support, just in case I needed to glance at it. A microphone was placed near my mouth, which meant I had to be quiet. Never knew when they'd turned it on or off.

It's funny, the puppeteer's life. Over the years, I have been under a miniature city street, performing a bus puppet; hidden within a church's communion table, ready to pop out and remind the kids about summer camp; or in my own stage, at a birthday party, holding two puppets in the air, trying to figure out how to get the family dog to stop sniffing my feet.

But here I was on set, with Linnie standing over me, her hand in the squirrel puppet, Milton, both of us waiting for the moment Miss Jo would walk over and talk to our characters.

*Backyard* had two days to shoot four episodes on two different sets. So there were no second chances. No retakes. If something happened—a forgotten line, a subpar performance, any kind of boo-boo—we just kept going. A lot of pressure? Yes. And we did our best to make it the best for our *Backyard* Buddies, our viewers across the country.

I could hear Miss Jo coming toward me, stepping across the plastic grass. She was talking about a new friend who had just moved into the yard.

I knew my lines from the script. I silently prepped, hearing C3PO's voice, reminding me he wasn't going that way, it was much too rocky. I felt the knock on the little door, and Ruben pushed it open.

I still couldn't see anything and could only go by what I heard. On most shows like this, a small monitor was placed next to the puppeteer so they could see how their movement looked to the camera. We didn't have monitors, so we performed the puppets as best we could.

It was hours of lying down or being scrunched under a table or standing around for long periods of time. It was holding puppets up while lighting was adjusted, and then shooting a scene, puppets up—heads down reading the script. This is basic TV puppetry.

Was it tiring? Yes. Was it fun? Yes! Did we make the big bucks, like the big shows? No. We volunteered, like the rest of the cast. But the payment was heavenly, eternal, far beyond mere dollars and cents.

Back to me and my rabbit. Miss Jo introduced herself politely. Ruben said the first line I ever said in a studio situation. He bowed in a stately fashion, and in the voice I've described, said,

"The pleasure of meeting the fair lady of this garden is all mine, indeed. I assure you."

———

Concentrating on getting it right, I didn't stop to think about the thousands of children who would be watching this episode when it was edited, finalized, and aired. But I knew something special was happening: an amazing, God-arranged opportunity.

As the years progressed, I took on more characters. I was Booker T. Worm, who enjoyed "consuming God's Word" as he popped up through a giant Bible, anchored to a desk with me underneath it. Opposite me was Bob Summers, also under the desk. He was Professor Piffle, who shared the episode's memory verse.

I was also a feisty Texas cowboy, Wild Bob. And later I performed a dad character (with a dadly mustache) in a puppet family. In the last months of the show, we introduced a flower named Flower. He would welcome the kids from behind the picket fence at the start of every episode.

But before Flower became part of the show, something momentous happened.

It involved a Bug.

*Oh the timing and the seasons of our lives.*
*Different houses, different people, different drives.*
*Sometimes we settle, then other times we roam,*
*And always the unquenchable desire for home.*

# Chapter 20
# VUG BUG

TRAFFIC LIGHTS OFFER THREE SELECTIONS: STOP. WAIT. GO. I've experienced them all.

Go: Graduation day at Southern California College. A big day. Stop: My mom didn't attend. She had attended my graduation from ANA, having just returned from Hawaii, her shoulders layered with Hawaiian leis. But she didn't come to my college graduation, due to one of her migraine headaches.

Mark and Bonnie to the rescue! A big Go! In a brilliant move, they picked up Mutti, and along with my nieces Jen and Jamie, attended the gathering of students, faculty, and family in the courtyard of the school's new administration complex. Pastor Jack Hayford gave the speech, we threw our hats to the Costa Mesa skies, and Wait: after searching around to find my own hat...my college days drew to a close. Stop.

Go: I drove home in my second car (the Ford Falcon having flown), a VW Super Beetle, sometimes called the Vug-Bug. So named because the letters VUG appeared in the license plate.

After this line of Volkswagens, the style was discontinued for several years. Unforgettable this Bug was, sporting a metallic green shell, round headlight eyes, and a slide-away roof. My brother Mark installed a radio for me, which turned out to be a good way to keep stamina on a long—make that *very* long—drive. But let me back up. In the story, not the VW.

Back in Sherman Oaks, living at home, I could not find any kind of ministry job, anywhere. My degree in biblical studies didn't seem to spring doors open as I thought it would. I contacted churches near and far, even the church in Urbana, Illinois, where Dick Foth was pastor. But he had moved on so that cancelled my reason for going there.

I volunteered at Calvary Chapel of Reseda as a youth pastor, and I didn't mind that there were only eight young people in the youth group and no pay. The experience was good. But I needed a real job. With pay. My humble bank account was dwindling.

Desperate, I found a job placement service in the phone book. After an interview, I got my first job. What a fiasco.

Every morning, I drove—well, crawled—through Los Angeles traffic to arrive at a large building downtown. The Reserve Insurance Company. At a desk, I organized thin, crinkly pieces of paper, thousands of them, in faded colors, ready to be filed away in big gray cabinets. But I worked at a snail's pace. My manager brought several ladies to my desk at the end of the week. At lightning speed they separated, organized, and filed. Meanwhile, I was still trying to pull apart duplicate pieces of paper. It didn't last very long.

A friend from The Church on the Way took me on at his company, CAMCO. Not too far from home, I worked in a storage room, boxing up extruded vinyl molding that later, inserted into chrome channeling, would make a cool car look much more cool—and protect against a swung open door that would dent metal but only bounced off the vinyl strip. Okay.

One bright spot was joining the Los Angeles Puppetry Guild, a chapter of the national Puppeteers of America. My timing was almost sensational. If I'd joined two months earlier, I would have been a puppeteer in *The Muppet Movie*. Puppeteers from the LA Guild were part of a giant wall of Muppet characters shown at the end of the movie. It would have been a very small part, ha ha, but a once-in-a-lifetime experience.

Years later, I applied and was accepted to attend a Muppet performance workshop in New York City, but had to turn it down. Looking back, it's okay, I would have many happy experiences with puppets on TV—or YouTube—in the years ahead.

But for now, I was puzzled. The Lord had led me to to ANA. To SCC. That led me to *Backyard*, which I was still doing, but it was not a paying job and only three days a month. Why couldn't I find a ministry-related job? I thought doors would open, since I knocked on a lot of them. Butler found himself stuck at the traffic signal, tapping on the steering wheel, foot on brake, yellow light glaring: Wait. Wait. Wait.

It was the first time I came face to face with the biggest little word in the Christian life.

I remember Pastor Dick Foth explaining it. He told the story of interviewing Elisabeth Elliott, a missionary, author, and speaker. Elisabeth's first husband, Jim Elliot, was killed in 1956 while attempting to share the gospel with the Auca people of eastern Ecuador. She would later return to that same tribe that killed her husband and spend two years among them, leading many to the Lord. Her story became widely known.

In the interview, Foth asked Elisabeth to put the whole of the Christian life into just one word. "That's easy, Mr. Foth," she said. "The word is trust."

BOOM! Small word. Huge impact.

I was trying to trust the Lord, really, but I was frustrated.

What did God want me to do? When would the Holy Spirit direct me?

I knew the Lord *would* lead me, but I didn't know when, where, or how.

Wait. That goes along with trust, doesn't it?

I didn't like waiting. Go was great. Stop was livable. Wait was no fun at all.

Foth went on to talk about a "trust walk," where one person is blindfolded and teamed up with another person. The two walk together for a while, the person without sight learning to trust the person who could see everything.

But then the blindfolded dude has to let go. He has to go on by himself, trusting the verbal commands of his former buddy, now standing a distance away. We all got the message. Foth had done this exercise at camps and retreats, so he knew how it went. The seeing person would say, "Turn left. Stop. Now go. Now turn right. Not too fast. You're doing good." Then he threw in a funny. "Oops. Yeah, that was a tree."

A tree was in my future too. Actually—lots of trees.

Since I was available, JoAn and Bob invited me to join them for the summer, working in their church in the Texas Hill Country. *Should I do it? Is this the Lord's will?*

Miss Jo also invited me to be part of the *Backyard* staff, illustrating a children's book, writing scripts, and helping as a kind of assistant producer. There was a paycheck, and room and board were free. And we'd be flying once a month to California to tape the four episodes. Everything sounded great to me. A job in ministry—but media ministry in particular. That was above and beyond what I'd hoped for, 'cuz again, I'd been prepared.

My mom was okay with it, even though she would go back to living alone. She'd done that for a long, long time. And after all, it was only for the summer. Or so I thought.

Summer with the Summers. Let's go!

So I packed my puppets and a few suitcases into Mort. Oh yeah, that was my Volkswagen's name. Mort, short for Morton. So named because, when I closed the driver's door, it went *CHUBB!* That sound could have been pulled from an album called *Touch*, by the electronic music composer Morton Subotnick, who made these chubb-type noises on his Buchla Synthesizer. Congratulations if you've ever heard of Buchla or Subotnick, which, come to think of it, does sound like two different people sneezing.

Off we went, Mort and me, following the Summers' directions written down on a piece of paper. No GPS, no Google maps in those days. I was driving across the United States, pursuing the Lord who so kindly brought me into his kingdom. The biggest road trip of my life.

Just me, Jesus, and Mark's radio.

> *"Trust and obey, for there's no other way,"*
> *So says the hymn from back in the day.*
> *It's timeless advice, for work and for play,*
> *"To be happy in Jesus, just trust and obey."*

# Chapter 21
# TREES AND A FLOWER

DRIVING AND DRIVING AND DRIVING.

Finally, I drove down the rugged, gravelly driveway to the Summers' Canyon Lake home. I'd never driven down a gravel driveway before. I worried about the tires popping. Or being quietly punctured and slowly deflating overnight. Silly, I know.

I pulled to a stop, opened the door, got out and stood up, stretching my legs.

Wait. What was that sound? Crickets? Cicadas? An undiscovered bug species?

Their chittering and chattering turned into a kind of tribal, jungle rhythm: swishing, clicking, rushing and then—roaring! There must have been thousands of the buggies hidden in the branches. The insectoid symphony would swell, crescendo, then diminish. Then rise again, surrounding me. Though I never saw the talented critters, anywhere. But here's what I did see.

A world of trees.

Trees in every direction, going on forever.

Trees and rocks and dirt and gurgling creek water.

It was beautiful, and of course, very organic. But very different.

I was a city mouse in a country mouse's environment. It was a new experience. And of course, as time went on, I grew to enjoy country life, nestled in God's creation.

The Summers welcomed me into their storybook house, where I had my own room and even a little brother, their son, Kip. In the years to follow, Kip and I would form a brotherly bond that would last a lifetime. Miss Jo cooked up delicious southern meals, and Bob played albums from his limitless supply of classical music recordings. He was a wealth of giftings, a writer, an artist, a pastor, and as I said, a man with music in his heart and soul.

In addition to my job for *BACKYARD*, I was able to help with the children in their church on Sundays, teaching the lesson alternately with Miss Jo, and of course the puppets were part of that experience, which brought that familiar, always comforting sound: children laughing.

Each weekday morning, I would meander down a trail to the small building where I had my office, a drawing board, and window-views of the foresty surroundings.

Canyon Lake was a long way from Sherman Oaks, but it began to feel like home. Not a replacement home, not a replacement family, but a place and a people to be at home with. My concept of home was stretched just a little bit more. It was good. And of course, Mort was at home there too. The Vug Bug and his tires were happy.

A few months after arriving in Canyon Lake, Mort and I made our way down the highway again, headed to the 1980 World Puppetry Festival in Washington, DC, at the Lincoln Center. It was, if I scrunched together all the adjectives I could into one word: spectacular.

You might not think of puppetry as being spectacular. I never did. That's because, mostly, in America, puppetry means talking-head puppets on TV or maybe a cute puppet show for a birthday party. But now I was seeing acts from all around the world. I saw:

*Figurentheater Triangel*, Henk Boerwinkel, from the Netherlands. Against a dark background, a scarecrow's jacket ripples in the wind. Suddenly it flips into a crow, squawking, snapping its beak.

*Sergei Obraztsov* (1901–1992), who stood behind a tall, slender puppet screen, and with his bare hands, topped by painted wooden ball-heads, performed a graceful, emotional ballet.

*Puppet Theater Puk* from Japan, featuring an umbrella dance, performed in bunraku, where a full-body character was moved by a concealed puppeteer cloaked in black.

*The Muppets* were there, too, along with puppet legends Shari Lewis and Lamb Chop and Burr Tillstrom, known for the TV show *Kukla, Fran, and Ollie.* At lunch I sat near Jim Henson, who sounded like his character, Kermit the Frog. I watched as he kindly signed his autograph on a piece of paper for a little boy.

What did I take away from this once-in-a-lifetime gathering?

That the main language of puppets should be movement.

MOVEMENT.

Their movement can be their language. They don't need to talk. Puppets would rather move and tell their story visually. All ages and languages can then understand it!

If the puppets *do* talk, the movement must reinforce the mood or message of the figure.

I also saw the importance of props. Props enhanced the story. There was something magical about a puppet picking up or moving around a prop. It reinforced their believability. Great for a one-man show like mine.

I was also drawn to building my own puppets. I'd been a store-bought puppet guy up to that point. But there was something special about making your own puppets. They were creations unique to their creator.

These revelations opened up new possibilities, both for comedy and Christian messages.

For example. A Styrofoam ball-on-a-stick, with a ragged robe, became Mr. Neebles. He picks a flower and gives it to a sad little finger puppet, who dances off with it. Then—out of nowhere—BOINGG! A fresh bouquet of flowers springs up, to Mr. Neebles' delight. The message? "Give, and it will be given to you. Good measure, pressed down, shaken together, running over, will be put into your lap" (Luke 6:38).

The flower puppet created for *Backyard* became my main character. I never could perform as a ventriloquist, so as Flower talked, moving his mouth, my mouth moved too. Somehow, instead of distracting, this actually became part of the act.

FLOWER: Um. Mr. Rod. Your mouth is moving while I'm talking. Stop that.

MR. ROD: I can't help it. It's how I bring you to life.

FLOWER: What do you mean, bring me to life?

MR. ROD: My hand is in you, making you talk. I give you your voice.

FLOWER: That's impossible! And may I say...weird!

MR. ROD: It's because you're a puppet.

FLOWER: A what-it?

MR. ROD: You're a puppet; I'm a puppeteer. My hand is in—

FLOWER: My head?

MR. ROD: In your life. I give you—your life.

FLOWER: How much do I owe you? Will you accept my garden card? Or dirt, maybe?

MR. ROD: No charge. It's all a gift.

FLOWER: Thank you, thank you. You're my...my...

MR. ROD: Your creator. Producer. Protector. And best friend.

FLOWER: Yeah...What's your name again?

You can see how a little puppet silliness can actually lead to a Bible lesson. A Scripture could have been added to drive the point home. Perhaps "My times are in your hand" (Psalm 31:15). Puppetry truly *can* lead to ministry.

For me it led to a lifetime of being a performer with unusual actors: gloves, tubes, foam shapes, a talking Flower, a talking dog named Arf, and for some reason, my most popular puppet sketch, "Don't Touch the Vacuum Cleaner."

In that skit, a furry purple monster is told not to touch the vacuum cleaner. He mocks the vacuum cleaner (really a flexible dryer hose with my arm inside), touching it several times, and because he has disobeyed the rules, he's swallowed up by the hose's suction power. (It's a trick, of course. I sweep the puppet down behind the curtain and it appears to have been swallowed.) Then the hose "spits the monster out," (the same trick in reverse) and he collapses, falling back below, relieved, and landing with a THUMMP that shakes the whole stage. A little skit based on Ephesians 6:1: "Children, obey your parents..."

After the show, I most always hear people singing the little song I made up, "Don't touch the vacuum cleaner!" Some people remember it many years later. I guess I'm a one-hit puppet-song boy-wonder.

Although one person did have something to tell me I didn't expect. "Thanks," the mom said, "for telling my kids they don't have to run the vacuum anymore."

Oops.

> *Chortles and giggles and giddiness with tears*
> *Laughter delights us, wiggles toes, tickles ears.*
> *It's the Bible's medicine for long dreary miles,*
> *"A merry heart does good," the book says and smiles.*

Chapter 22
# OUR FIRST HOME

REMEMBER THAT HOUSE I PASSED AS A CHILD? THE HOUSE with the lady and the music inside?

Fast forward to the year 1980. In the twenty-fifth year of my life, Pastor Allen Randolph invited me to join the staff of Trinity Church in San Antonio as junior high pastor and graphic artist, which translates, church bulletin-maker.

Previous to that, *Backyard* had been cancelled by TBN, apparently due to the cost of production. The Summers had moved on from their church in Canyon Lake, and we had visited Trinity Church for several Sundays.

On the very first Sunday, I noticed a cute girl playing the piano as part of the worship team. It was, as I described it many years back, real piano music, in a very large living room. Ha ha, a house with a lady and music inside. Maybe that was a prophetic prelude to a reality so many years later!

Eventually, there was a transition from my life with the Summers family, and I accepted the position at the church. Though I'd been away from home for several years, this seemed to make it certain that I was not moving back to California.

It didn't come as a shock to anyone since I'd been gone for so long. But I still had to tell my people that I was permanently relocating. A big step. Halfway across the country.

I called my mom, and I kept in touch with Mark and Bonnie. Mutti wrote me sweet letters with her signature blue fountain pen on light blue stationery. Often a little check would be included.

Again, home had changed. New locations, new faces, and new work.

I guess it's kind of a normal thing for a young adult person, but as I think back, it was a sacrifice in a way, staying in Texas with my family and my friends so far away.

I felt I did the right thing. It was an act of faith, like Abraham going out, not knowing where he was going. I didn't know what the future would hold.

I'd stepped out several times now. Or stepped up really, like a person boarding a magic carpet, with no ticket, no (apparent) pilot, and all around him, the vast expanse of the sky. It reminds me of one of my favorite animated movies, *Aladdin*.

Remember when Aladdin stands on the flying carpet, looking at Princess Jasmine? She places her hand on the edge of the rug and asks, "Is it safe?"

Aladdin leans over toward her and extends his hand. "Sure! Do you trust me?"

That's almost a picture of the Christian life, isn't it? The Lord, elevated to a higher level than mere human beings, offers an elevated life, an abundant, fulfilling life, but there's a question: Do we trust him?

For some reason, I hear Kevin's puppets in chapel at SCC, singing in that nasally voice, "Do you trust him?"

I believe I did. I moved into an apartment with a friend, moved into an office at the church, and a new life began. But I had seen a princess. That first time we visited Trinity Church. I saw her playing the palace instrument, a grand piano. I thought she was cute, too cute for me. But as if a higher power—the Holy Spirit—

was reaching out to me—in the form of a push—I decided to take a chance.

A fellow staff member, Mitch Silvia, knew her family, so he said he would introduce me to Jeri Green. Mitch and I made a plan for after church. Mitch would talk to the family, and I would slip up casually. That didn't work exactly. I walked up. That part worked.

But Mitch was involved talking to her brother about basketball or something. *Mitch! I'm standing here! Mitch!* Now that I stood closer, I noticed she was even more cute than I had thought. But it was getting awkward with me just standing there. Mitch is a great guy, of course, a real people-person, which makes him a great pastor. And, of course, finally:

Mitch turned around. "Oh, hey Rod. Jeri, this is Rod. Rod, this is Jeri Green."

Now. I'm not sure how to explain what happened next. I heard a voice. Not next to me, but in my head. Yes, it was like the night back in '72 when I sensed the Lord speaking to me. It was that kind of inner voice again. But the statement was one of those ton-of-bricks statements.

"You've just met your wife."

I immediately thought, *That's not the Lord! That's wishful thinking. She's way too cute for me. Forget the thought. Forget it!*

All of that happened in a split second as I was looking at Jeri Green. I never told anybody about it, of course.

Life went on. And we did become friends.

Jeri was working at Frost Bank at the time, having just graduated from the University of Texas at San Antonio. We enjoyed our friendship.

I let her borrow my jazz albums, those being Pat Metheny, Gary Burton, and Chick Corea. She, in turn, let me borrow her gospel albums, Andraé Crouch and Walter Hawkins and the Hawkins Family. We also enjoyed going to the McNay Art Museum and talking about the wonderful, diverse works displayed in that old-fashioned mansion, nestled away in downtown San Antonio.

During that time, as you might expect, I fell in love. And, I suppose, she fell in like. We were friends for a long time, with no sign of the relationship developing into dating or romance. So after nearly two years and feeling discouraged, I broke it off. At the water fountain in the church lobby. "I guess I need my albums back," I started, and explained the friendship was going away, although I'd give her albums back as well, of course. I thought I saw a tear, a moisture around her eyes, but didn't understand why that would be happening...

After a few months, she sent a letter, with a poetic message that let me know she was interested in being more than friends. And so we got back together. This time, as sweethearts.

About a year later, she walked down the aisle, my beautiful bride. We were married by Pastor Randolph, May 19, 1984. I was twenty-nine. Jeri was twenty-four.

My mom, Mark and Bonnie (with Jen and Jaime), Brian Horner, Jenny Smith, and other dear friends came from California to attend. All in all, the church was full, and I remember running out of cake and punch. Also that my rental shoes didn't match; one shoe was a size and a half too small. During the ceremony I thought, *What is wrong with my left foot?*

Jeri and I moved into a small apartment, then a small home, and a few years later welcomed our first child, a baby boy. God is good.

In this home, this small yet cozy home, I had a wife. She had a knack for decorating, as well as cooking and garden making. And of course, piano playing. Yes, in the living room.

So now I had a family. Home was again redefined, broadened and deepened, and made even more wonderful.

Mutti was not able to travel, but we visited her with little Jonathan. Now in a retirement home, she met her first great-grandson and played with him, a little game she did with her fingers that made him smile.

We continued to send her pictures and receive letters. Eventually the letters stopped coming, and I got a phone call.

In Southern California, a small group gathered for Mass. I sat with my mom, Uncle Werner (Mutti's son), wishing it were St. Cyril's, wishing it weren't happening. Wishing I'd visited her more, called her more.

She often said, and it bothered me, "Dear, I vill not alvays be with you." True, yet not true. Her memory is so sweet, so deep and so strong, she will never really go away. She *is* always with me.

Happy to say, so many in my life knew her, including Jeri, and in a small way, Jonathan. Coming back home to my wife and little boy was a genuine comfort.

Around that time, another member of our family arrived, if I can put it that way. Let me announce: The TASCAM PortaStudio Mini One four-track cassette recorder. Tah dah! Just let those beautiful words pan across the expanse of this little page.

Yes, ladies and gentlemen, multitrack recording had come home. No longer would professional studios be the only place to find recording equipment that would allow multiple tracks. By that I mean, when recording a song, you could lay down drums, then bass, then guitars, and so on, overlapping the tracks.

Now there was an affordable recorder, in a small green box, that would do four passes (four tracks) or more. On cassette. Not the highest quality in the world, but with careful recording and mixing, it would sound pretty good.

I'd could play drums and I'd noodled around on keyboards here and there. Now I had a way to make layered recordings, just goof-around music, in my spare time. Yessss!

But God had another plan.

And as always, a greater plan. And its time had come.

Since I could be rather dense and often preoccupied, he chose to speak in a way I couldn't miss. From my wife. And her funny best friend.

*We know this about our God: He always has a plan.*
*And this, we know, is also true: He will likely use a man.*
*Of course, by that, I mean to say: He uses ladies too.*
*We all say yes and follow. There is a lot of work to do.*

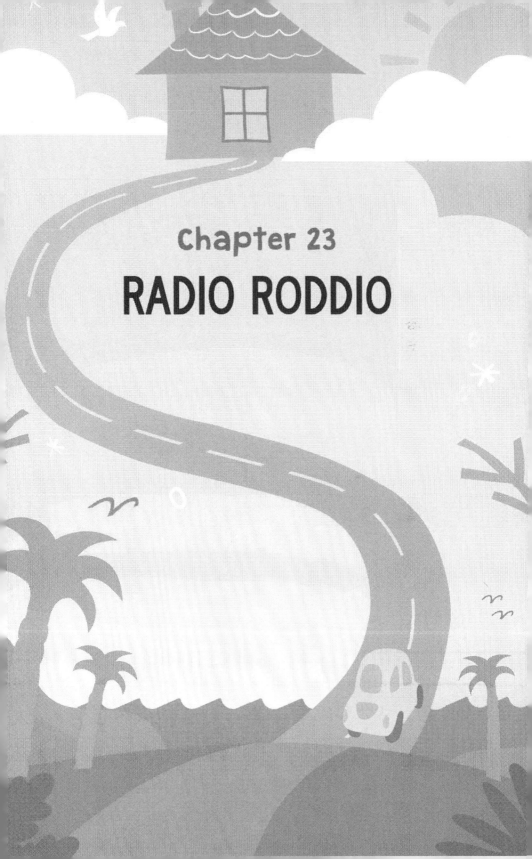

# Chapter 23
# RADIO RODDIO

Here's how to make a weekly church bulletin in the 1980s. Brace yourself.

1. Write your articles on the typewriter.
2. Get articles from the other staff members.
3. Get your articles proofed for errors.
4. Keep asking staff for their articles. Beg if necessary.
5. Politely make sure the pastor is working on his article.
6. Demand the staff respond or their articles will *not* be in the bulletin.
7. Immediately receive all articles from the staff. Except the music guy.
8. Have the final copy typed so it will fit into the columns.
9. Using hot wax, adhere the carefully cut paper to the layout sheet.
10. Before showing it to the printer, show it to the pastor.
11. Redo the entire process for the articles the pastor has rewritten.
12. Face the printing lady who needs the copy and artwork NOW!

And that was just Tuesday. Truth is, I enjoyed my job, with its balance between doing graphics and being a pastor to young people. I pastored junior highers, then high schoolers, then the whole youth group. Then switched to young couples, and finally, ironically, toward the end of the sixteen years, I served as children's pastor. That's a lot of bulletins!

On the side I wrote children's stories and submitted them for publication. Which should read, "I wrote children's stories." Because I never did publish any, and eventually only a few articles here and there.

On another side, the puppet ministry was going strong, both within the church and to other churches and libraries.

Add to that the joy of our growing family, eventually with three children, two boys and one girl.

But the truth is, we were restless. More and more so as the years wore on.

*Could there be something else for us?* Like the song "Somewhere Out There," from the animated film *An American Tale* (1986), Jeri and I were drawn to begin looking for something else. Something more. Somewhere. Anywhere.

We checked out a Christian television station in Concord, California. But I'd be walking around with a heavy camera on my shoulder.

Visited American Family Radio in Tupelo, Mississippi. I'd be doing audio production, but the same old thing over and over.

Then on to Focus on the Family, where I interviewed for a producer spot on the James Dobson radio broadcast. They felt I was overqualified. I felt let down. Because...

That was the last door. And it was locked.

About that time, Jeri's best friend Rhonda came by to see us, and in her cheery way, she reminded me that, "Sometimes when God closes a door, he opens a window." That funny phrase seemed to be highlighted with a heavenly marker. I understood it, but we had been searching diligently—there were no other openings out there.

Then came another heavenly-highlighted statement. Jeri said, "Why don't you use your puppet voices and your four-track recorder to create a radio show?"

Brilliant. What a great idea! (I just wrote that now. It's not what I said then.)

"That's an interesting idea, but how would I do that? What would it be about? How long would it take? I mean, what characters would I use, and what radio station, in what state, would ever want to air such a thing?"

I sat in the lobby of KSLR, a Christian radio station in San Antonio, just down the freeway from the church.

In my hand was a cassette tape in a plastic box labeled *FunLight Radio*. I'd worked on the fifteen-minute demo for around six months.

Flower and Mr. Rod were the hosts, along with Pete Dah Spidah, Torkie the Red Cow, Professor Veinersnitzel, Ageless Oak, Beep the Master-Word Computer, and a little rhyming story, Teeny Tiny Tales. I liked it pretty well but wasn't sure how this would play out if I had to have a new one every week. How to crunch down six months into one week? And do that week after week after week?

Bob Lepine, the general manager, came out to meet me. He knew of me through a mutual friend, so he was open to giving the show a listen. I explained a little about my puppet ministry. Handed him the demo cassette. He took it. We said good-bye.

The second visit rolled around, and he liked it. He wanted to air it. I smiled, but inside I was like, *Oh NOOOOO! How can I do one a*

189

*week?* And yet spiritually, a calming *Thank you, Lord. Here's a chance to reach a lot of kids. And be funny at the same time!*

*FunLight* went into production, with me working 4:00 a.m. to 7:00 a.m., trying to perform and record—quietly—in the living room. One time I had to have a character jump from a height into a pool of water or something, so trying to be quiet, I yelled, "AHHHHH-HHHHHHH!" softly. But not softly enough. Our little boy came out, rubbing his eyes, a bit confused, asking, "Daddy?"

Pastor Randolph was not only fine with me doing the show, he asked if I would turn it into a Wednesday night service just for the kids. *FunLight Kids Club.* I dreamed up an attic and an old-time radio, oversized, into which I could secure a cassette player, to give the kids a preview of that Saturday's radio show.

Now I could dream up a big radio. But I could never build one.

Enter Chester Stevens.

Remember Grandad Harrel? Well, God brought another older-than-me gentleman into my life. Another blessing of being in God's family, nestled in a church home.

Chester was a master craftsman, with a garage workshop, huge array of tools, and the skills to build anything. He built the large radio, and it was beautiful, like a Hollywood movie prop.

But he made me learn a few skills too. Real advanced stuff: hammer a nail. Pull out the bent-up nail. Hammer in a new nail—correctly. Same with a screwdriver. Even pliers. And these were all skills I would need down the road as we made improvements to our houses through the years.

After the Chester-built radio came the *FunLight* attic.

The attic was a large, colorful set on wheels, built by Chester and other woodworkers in the church. All done without pay, for the sake of building up kids in God's Word and ways.

At the end of the weekly kids' service, the attic set was wheeled back into a large closet at one end of the basketball court in the Family Center and the corrugated door pulled down.

I never thought that *FunLight* would become an actual place kids could visit each week. That little radio show was expanding!

That's when I heard from Dodd Morris at The Children's Sonshine Network. They wanted the show and would broadcast it beyond San Antonio. Then people from American Family Radio (where I had visited) picked it up, and—amazingly—the little show produced on four-track cassette was now nationally syndicated as far as Haiti.

I received lots of mail every week, sending out stickers, bookmarks, coloring pages, a puzzle book, and finally, The Daily Bulb, a one-page newspaper, which introduced a superhero, Captain FunLight. He would leap into the sky, flying into adventure, calling out, "Time to shine!"

And it was time to shine. But not in San Antonio anymore.

> *Why is it, that home is a place we must leave?*
> *When to its cares and comforts we so long to cleave?*
> *Jesus lived on earth without a house, pillow, or bed,*
> *He lived as though homeless, no place to lay his head.*
> *Then he ascended, to heaven's glory beyond compare,*
> *And prepares us a dwelling place, to live with him there.*

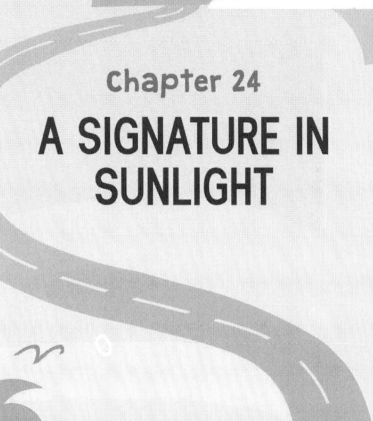

# Chapter 24
# A SIGNATURE IN SUNLIGHT

STORM CLOUDS AHEAD...

In 1774, William Cowper wrote a hymn, "God Moves in a Mysterious Way." Jeremy Riddle recently recorded it, and the first stanza goes like this:

> *God moves in a mysterious way*
> *His wonders to perform.*
> *He plants His footsteps in the sea*
> *And rides upon the storm.*

The Lord does move in mysterious, wonderful, wind-driven ways. I believe the opposite truth as well: The Lord speaks through everyday occurrences.

Jeri and I searched for a long time but could not find another church or media opening for me. *FunLight* aired every Saturday morning, getting good responses from listeners. I kept writing children's stories that slept in file folders. We continued at Trinity Church, but now the search had intensified.

Now we were driving to the Dallas-Fort Worth metroplex—again—to check on open doors or upraised windows. At last! we found some. Three, in fact.

ONE: The Summers were pastoring in Dallas and needed a bulletin writer/editor.

TWO: A Christian video game producer offered me a large amount of voice-over work.

THREE: A Fort Worth media company liked a video game I'd written for *Integrity Music*, *Attack of the Tune Twister,* and talked to me about turning it into an animated series.

Three good opportunities! Not exactly a full-time job with benefits, but we felt it could work. I did ask the Lord for some kind of sign, and I believe he gave us one.

Driving in the minivan, we were stunned by a grouping of storm clouds, pierced through by golden beams. A spectacular sunrise. Jeri and I took it to be God's signature in sunlight, a "Yes" from the Lord. It qualified as mysterious and everyday, implying, "Move to DFW."

But thinking back now, knowing how the story played out, the elements of the sunrise were more specific than I realized. It was a sunrise with a hint of trouble.

The brilliant beams where shining through stormy clouds.

Sure enough, a stormy season would be part of our future.

Yet the light would shine through. And carry us through, to the fullness of the next sunrise: a whole new kind of ministry. For kids.

Oops. Spoilers.

We left Trinity Church after sixteen years of service. I arrived single and left married with three kids, Jonathan, Julian, and Benjamin. Saying good-bye was difficult. Uprooting the family was even harder.

On Thanksgiving Day 1998, we arrived at the house we had purchased some weeks before in Arlington, halfway between Dallas and Fort Worth. We gradually settled in, enrolled the kids in public school, and I set up my audio studio, jumping into the large amount of voice-over scripts for *Onesimus*, the video game.

Over several weeks, I recorded, edited, and finally sent the audio files. And then waited. And waited. I made several calls—but I never heard back. Ever.

My next source of income, the media company interested in the *Tune Twister* series, decided all they could do was a one-minute commercial for the *Integrity* game. I did narrate it, but that was that. One small paycheck.

Thankfully, I did get to work with the Summers, laying out their Sunday bulletin and editing a book for Miss Jo. But, as agreed, that was a part-time position.

So, there we were. A five-person family with two cars, a house, and a small income. The stormy clouds. Yet God took care of us. The golden beams! We never missed a payment, never were in need, and managed to have presents for the three funnies (kids) under the Christmas tree.

A year passed.

I looked for other work, even puppet shows, but nothing opened up. And then, as Jeri's friend Rhonda had said—or more accurately, prophesied, a window opened. A car window. Cue the sound effect: *ZZZZZ-CLINK.* Radio waves floated into the minivan and emerged as music from the car speakers. Our daughter spun the dial to her favorite station.

Radio Disney.

Now *FunLight Radio* was pre-produced. Radio Disney was LIVE and interactive. Kids called in, requested songs, played games, and most importantly—won prizes, going crazy with happiness! Then the jingle slogan played, "Radio Disney. We're all ears!"

I was all ears too. Why not a LIVE Christian radio show for kids? Christian kids' music was popular, as well as Christian kids' books and videos. Yet nothing like that existed for kids and families, as far as I knew.

Dallas-Fort Worth had lots of Christian radio stations. Hmmm.

I had to face that same old *How could I do that?* thought, but financial need gave me a boost. I created a rough demo, with the music/games/prizes format, then contacted three stations. They all said no.

Later, one of those, a nonprofit station, KCBI, called back, and after some months hired me to work in promotions, going to places and events to set up a tent and represent the station...but also as director of children's programming, in charge of a four-hour kids' block every Saturday morning. Yes, you guessed it. The golden beams. Golden broadcast beams!

I had six months to prepare a theme and overarching format, utilizing the shows they already had in place but adding the music, games, and prizes. And I called it:

*KidZone Radio*

Station Manager Ron Harris felt that this radio show filled a gap in children's programming.

> "There was a need for creative programming for young people. Then came Rod Butler and *KidZone Radio*. I remember one crazy activity where the kids were to jump off a diving board and quote Scripture before splashing into the water. The parent was to call in and chronicle the event.

Honestly, I thought no one would do that. But the phones lit up, and call after call was put on the air. Crazy? Yes, but young people were memorizing God's Word, and that would stay with them long after the craziness was gone."

*KidZone Radio* premiered on January 1, 2000, the day known as Y2K. News reports warned that all the computers in America—or maybe the whole world—would suddenly shut down. Okay, that made me nervous. Then—we had a mini-Y2K right there in the control room where I would be doing the show. The computer didn't shut down, but...

All the music, features, sound effects—everything I had prepared—was not showing up on the studio computer! Dave Jolly, my control board operator, was calm. I was borderline hysterical, though subdued, of course. I thought, *THIS CAN'T BE HAPPENING!* But I said, calmly, "Uh, Dave, what should we do?" The clock ticked toward our start time, minutes away.

Dave was experienced. He called an engineer, shuffled around a few of the existing programs to buy us time, and in an hour we were operational. But there was something else to shiver about.

This was LIVE radio. I was on the air, *LIVE*. I couldn't stop the broadcast, rewind, and do three or four more takes as I had with *FunLight*. If I messed up, I messed up. There was no tape delay like commercial stations have. I had a MUTE button for a sneeze or a hiccup. But other than that, what I said—went out there. And that took some getting used to.

As the months rolled on, I calmed down, got crazier, and watched as the little red lights on the phone lit up with callers. From across the metroplex, kids called in to play games like Mystery Bible

Theater, Quiz Kidz, Name That Song, and Humming the Hymns with Linguini Fettuccini (you know, the famous opera singer, ha ha).

Or they requested music by Jump5, Shout Praises Kids, or Go Fish. They hoped to win a prize—really any kind of prize—be it CDs, videos, books, or event tickets. And they screamed with joy when I proclaimed, "You're a winner in the *KidZone!*"

Doing the show involved a team, who would become like a family. The crew for the show included me, a board op, and two phone producers, and we all bonded through the experience.

And when it came to testimonies from the kids, the show went to a higher zone.

"Daddy went to heaven about two weeks ago," a young listener told me, "and when I really miss him, Mama lets me hold the sweater he used to wear, and it smells good, like my daddy, and I feel better. That's my God story."

I loved meeting the kids and families in person. We often set up a table at a Christian bookstore, and I interacted with listeners, sometimes recording a shout-out they would later hear on air. I'd give away coloring pages and pens and stickers.

One year at the Texas State Fair we gave away clear bouncy balls with the *KidZone* logo inside. We didn't just hand those out, we *bounced* them out to kids who caught them!

At these kind of events, kids didn't know what I looked like, so sometimes, well, it was a revelation.

At a Bible book store, a little boy asked if I was KZ Rod. I said yes. He looked up at his mother and said, "Mom, he's so *old!*"

*The disciples shooed the little children away,*
*When the kids were brought to Jesus one day.*
*The Master insisted, "Bring the children to me."*
*Living close to Jesus is the best place to be!*

# Chapter 25
# COCONUTTY!

Again I was called into an office. This time, by the manager of the radio station.

Ron Harris looked at me from across his desk, smiling. He was pleased with the Saturday morning response and the ratings and wanted to syndicate the show. Wow. I knew that would have the potential to reach more kids, but I had no idea how it would happen.

Ron was very involved in the National Religious Broadcasters (NRB) and had connections to lots of other stations. He knew how to make it happen. And, since we discovered that the name *KidZone* was already trademarked, we needed to create a new name. We also needed about, oh, ten thousand dollars for equipment, materials, and a new broadcast studio. Gulp.

Next thing I knew I was back in the control room (the main broadcast studio) at five thirty on a Friday morning, with Ron prepping me as a guest on his show. His goal was to use *The Morning Show*, about three hours long, to raise the ten thousand dollars. Gulp again. This man had faith. He also had a great sense of humor, a deep love for Scripture, and a soft spot for children.

His eyes twinkled, and his voice was strong. "I'll be driving it," he explained. "I'll toss it to you for comments. Talk briefly—no more than a minute. And don't mention money. Leave that to me." No argument there.

The show kicked in. There was the usual music and traffic reports and encouragement, mixed with a steady drive asking listeners to give. The phones were ringing. Volunteers, spread out across the lobby, were answering.

A few minutes before the end of the program, we hit our goal—and then exceeded it.

Even after *The Morning Show* was over, the phones kept ringing! It was exciting—downright amazing—I'd never seen anything like it. The heart of listeners to give toward that group of people Jesus called "the greatest in the kingdom" (Matthew 18:4): kids.

Now things got busy. Engineers and power tools at work.

An old broadcast room was gutted. From that a new broadcast room was built. Cabinets and equipment installed. Satellite availability secured. Even a toll-free number created that you could remember as numbers—and as a clever choice of words. All of this revolved around the idea, the concept, the word that came to me a few weeks prior.

*Coconut.*

Which didn't really work by itself. So I added:

*Hut.*

Which, looking online, was already taken. So I added:

*Radio.*

That seemed to cut off abruptly. So I added:

*Show.*

*The Coconut Hut Radio Show.*

A mouthful. But a delicious one.

I became Bongo Rod. Pete Dah Spidah's voice became Bob Dah Lobstah's voice. We added Coco and Nutt (brother and sister coconuts), a CocoBot, and Finny the Fish. I created the games and gathered the prizes, and a Dallas jingle company created a slammin' jingle.

And the phone number, after months of searching and changing, was:

1-888-I-AM-A-NUT which is the same as 1-888-426-2688.

The first Saturday rolled in with a splash on May 14, 2005.

Our Coconutty crew gathered for a pre-show meeting around six every Saturday morning. The next four hours on the air combined music from popular kid/youth Christian music groups including Jump 5, Mission Six, The Rubyz, TobyMac, and more. Kids requested songs, won prizes, talked about their faith, and like with *KidZone*, kids gave the show its splash, sparkle, and shine.

But since the callers were kids, things were...unpredictable. There were unexpected moments. I had to think fast. And keep a straight face. Even though it was radio.

I remember talking to Tommy. Live on the air. *LIVE.* On the air. With lots of people listening.

"Hi, Bongo Rod!" Tommy chimed.

"Hey, Tommy. Watcha doin'?"

"I'm on the potty!"

PAUSE. I try to recover quickly and figure out what to say.

"Well, I hope everything works out okay," I say. Like, that was *not* the thing to say.

PAUSE while I try—again—to recover quickly. From my own blunder.

"So what are you calling about?" I ask casually.

"I want to hear Veggie Tales!"

"Okay, great. What song?"

"The one with the singing peas."

I cringed at the word "pea," connecting it to the recent word, potty, but of course, he didn't intend any kind of a double meaning. It was just another hilarious, totally spontaneous moment. With kids.

Those moments were balanced out by meaningful, heart-touching interactions. I remember when Ariel talked about standing up for her little brother and saving him from a threatening bully. And other kids who answered Bible quiz questions or talked very openly about how God was working in their lives.

These kinds of conversations happened because our phone producers knew how to talk to callers and prep them for going on air. Sometimes the kids were bashful, barely audible. Other times they couldn't stop talking. Surfin' Sarah remembers a funny conversation.

SURFIN' SARAH: *Coconut Hut Radio Show*, Surfin' Sarah speaking.

CALLER: Surfin' Sarah!

SURFIN' SARAH: Hi! And who's this?

CALLER: It's me! (PAUSE) Don't you remember me?

SURFIN' SARAH: Um, I think so...

(The time ticks away. She needs to get two callers for the game in two minutes.)

CALLER: It's Johnny! Remember? You want to hear about my basketball game?

Sarah recalls those mornings:

> "The show was like a family; it was a place where I felt like I belonged. I'm so honored to be part of this Coconutty family, surrounded by the love of Christ that shined through everyone who worked on the show. It still shines to this day!"

There are so many more stories to recount, but I'm overwhelmingly grateful to have been part of that ministry. Just the other day I received an email from a listener many years after the show had been discontinued.

> Hey, Bongo Rod! Your show had such an incredible impact on me growing up. I felt like I had my own radio show that was geared toward my age group. I just wanted you to know, you made an impact for Christ.

I was on the air for nearly fourteen years with *KidZone* and *Coconut Hut*. Twenty-five years if you count *FunLight Radio*. It felt like all of those years culminated in the final show.

That last *Coconut Hut Radio Show* was a tough one. KCBI was going through all kinds of changes, and eventually, they would make Saturday mornings music oriented, with only an hour of pre-recorded kids' shows starting at six in the morning. This turned out to be the last Saturday with the four-hour block for children.

Thankfully, we were able to tell listeners it was the last show. A lot of radio shows just disappear. You tune to the same frequency—and it's something completely different. But making that announcement brought its own challenges.

The phone lines went crazy, as did email, website, Facebook, and text. Parents were upset and kids very disappointed. But on the air, with the sweet testimonies and thankfulness of the kid listeners, and with music, games, and prizes, the show went on, as they say. And then sadly, it went off. But we went off with a special closing moment.

The Veggie Tales characters had recorded their own version of a famous Roy Rogers song. We closed with it every Saturday on *KidZone* and played it regularly on *Coconut Hut*. It was doubly impacting for me, since my late father had written several Roy Rogers movies.

It was the end of a beautiful season. The happy echoes continued for some time. In fact, as I write this, one of those echoes plays on. Larry the Cucumber singing for Roy Rogers:

"Happy trails to you, till we meet again..."

> *Spring is the season for new growth and light,*
> *Summer is sunshine and warm wind for kites.*
> *Autumn is sundown, with a chill in the breeze,*
> *Winter is snowfall and bare branches on trees.*

Chapter 26

# INTO WINTER

SITTING AT THE COMPUTER. TRYING TO FIND EMPLOYMENT.

The middle of summer. Long days. Texas heat. And once again this feeling, these thoughts: *What kind of job can Rod Butler do? He can do voices but not numbers. He can write, but not professionally. He can perform, but that's not steady pay.* Note: It's never a good idea to list all the things you can't do. Besides, the list of things you *can* do is always longer.

I spent hours searching online. Calling radio stations. Updating my resume. And when I needed a break, I went through my many books of scribbled-down poetry, thinking about making a compilation one day. Or looked at my little toy collection. Then back to the job hunt.

But there was an anchor point.

Home.

Being out of work made me grateful to have a home.

It was a stable place in a time of career instability. And I'm thankful to say, it was a beautiful home, with a floor plan designed by my wife. We also had a church home, with believers who were surrounding us in prayer.

This non-working period lasted about six months—but it felt like years.

Outside: the hot months of summer. Inside: my cold personal winter. Seriously, I fought a kind of desperation. I felt unemployable. Down deep, kind of worthless. Hopeless.

Around me, digital technology and social media changed the look, feel, and functionality of just about everything. I felt out of sync and didn't want to learn more about websites, blogs, and passwords to catch up with the younger generation. My feelings turned from discouragement to a brand of middle-aged isolation.

I wonder. Does the enemy of our faith look for times like these to isolate us, then circle up, stalk, and pounce? Jesus fought demons. Peter forsook the Lord. Paul struggled with pain and unanswered prayers for relief. What was going on?

Paul wrote to the Ephesians about an invisible reality: a war against cosmic powers and "spiritual forces of evil in the heavenly places" (Ephesians 6:12) and then instructed believers to take up their armor. I'd like to say I did that. I know I prayed. But I credit the Lord for being patient with me, and one day, sending a new season in the sound of a phone call. You could say, the opening of another window. A call I didn't make—a window I didn't even know about.

"Rod, you're a writer, aren't you?" asked Phil Hall, who used to run the board for me at KCBI. "I work for Responsive Ed, and they're looking for writers."

I'd never written for education, but I jumped at the chance. I drove about an hour from the house to their headquarters for an interview and found out I'd actually be writing scripts for animated videos. Cool! I mean, amazing, and so out of the blue. It's true: if you don't find the answer, be patient, the answer may find you.

A new season began—with a point of affirmation I'll never forget.

As a new employee of Responsive Education Solutions, I had to wear a badge. A clip-on badge with a little happy book character on it. Its springy arms were outstretched, as if announcing my name. And my title.

Rod Butler
Script Writer

I was about to make my living by writing scripts. You know that made a deep connection in me, with my dad writing scripts. Those were movies, these would be videos, but the great thing: This was work. Work with words. With sentences and paragraphs and watching those become animated videos. Not just for entertainment but for education too. And sometimes a blending of those together. And a paycheck, every two weeks. My Lord.

We're never too young or too old in God's timing, in the Holy Spirit's way of doing things. Psalm 8:2 seems to speak of infants doing spiritual warfare: "Out of the mouth of babies and infants, you have established strength because of your foes, to still the enemy and the avenger." Psalm 148:12–13 calls out to all ages, "Young men and maidens together, old men and children! Let them praise the name of the LORD..."

Super Bowl V winner Tommy Maxwell once said to me, "God can use anybody to do anything." You said it, Tommy. And my mother-in-law, Nancy Green, in her eighties, topped it off with "At any time!"

About that time, other scripts of mine were becoming short cartoons. Let me back up.

As a kid in Sherman Oaks (Oh no—another kid in Sherman Oaks story!), I remember the tall office buildings rising into the landscape of our small, snuggly town. You know, the little town with Kerry's and Denny's.

One evening, riding in back seat of the car, I looked out the window at a searchlight, blazing a bright beam that swept the sky like a powerful force, searching out wrongdoers in the murky shadows. Well. Probably just advertising a Ralph Williams or Cal Worthington used-car lot.

And when we drove past the actual light, a large canister-shaped projector, I could hardly look at the brilliance of that beam.

Many years later, *FunLight Radio* came along, and with it came a comical superhero, Captain FunLight. And from him, Captain FlashLight, who, with an over-the-top Buzz Lightyear-type voice, would announce himself to a dark-doer, saying, "It is I, Captaaaaaaaain FlashLight!"

During the KCBI days, I began a nonprofit business, Filament City Media, and dear people from our church at the time, Grace Community Church, donated funding for me to make my first cartoon.

At the same church, on a graduation Sunday, down at the front where the senior students gathered, I prayed for a high school graduate named Parker who wanted to get into animation. He had amazing talent, and we made a demo video based on a miniseries from Coconut Hut, *The Brilliant Adventures of Captain FlashLight*.

Once again I have to say: If it had not been for my church family and my church home, well, many significant things in my life and career would not have happened.

We continued to develop *Captain FlashLight*, but due to the expense involved, we switched to a more simple cartoon idea: a boy and his dog, creating a new series of one-minute shorts called *Boy +*

*Dog.* Through my connections with the National Religious Broadcasters, I had a few TV networks interested in airing it.

So even in my season of winter, I was able to launch the animated series *Boy + Dog*, with twelve episodes that aired on Daystar Television, a few other places, and—coming full circle—TBN.

And zooming ahead to 2021, when my puppets became a YouTube Channel, *Rod the Puppet Guy* (www.youtube.com/RodThePup petGuy), who should sneak in through the doggie door? Cal the BOY and Ollie the DOG and a sampling of their episodes picking up some views so many years later.

Funny how these things happen. I guess you could say, if we are planted, we will grow. And if we're planted in good soil, we can yield abundant productivity. And by "planted," I mean planted in a family of believers. And from that planting, watch the goodness that sprouts up all around you.

> "The righteous flourish like the palm tree and grow like a cedar in Lebanon. They are planted in the house of the LORD; they flourish in the courts of our God. They still bear fruit in old age; they are ever full of sap and green, to declare that the LORD is upright; he is my rock, and there is no unrighteousness in him" (Psalm 92:12–15).

> *The hummingbird builds her nest in the tree,*
> *The tree is a fortress to a bird such as she.*
> *She settles and mothers, and the baby birds grow,*
> *Grown then and wing-strong, she watches them go.*

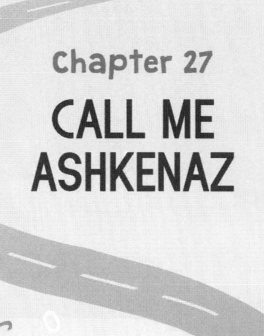

# Chapter 27

# CALL ME ASHKENAZ

One day my past invaded my present. And Facebook flipped my future.

In September of 2015, the funny journey found my wife and me standing at Terminal 2 at the Vaclav Havel airport in the Czech Republic. The invitation came from my second cousin Christian Lederer in Hamburg, Germany. He had contacted me on Facebook with news about my Aunt Marketa.

> Dear Rod, we learned that Marketa died this morning. Finally she could go peacefully without pain. The funeral of Marketa will be on Friday, Sept. 4th on the Jewish Cemetery of Teplice at the old Lederer family grave. We would be just thrilled if somebody of your Mutti's branch of the family tree would join us. Love, Christian.

Aunt Marketa Freund was the daughter of Henriette Horenovsky, the sister of my grandmother, Maria Koppl. I had seen Aunt Henriette and Aunt Marketa two or three times across my life, but this would be an unrepeatable experience, so I told Christian we would be there.

But something wasn't right. Christian, admittedly our family's young historian, must have made a mistake. I read part of the message again.

> ...the Jewish Cemetery of Teplice...

It said *Jewish*. But no one in our family was Jewish. We were all Catholic, right? Mutti—for sure. I responded, questioning, and of course, he was not wrong.

"Your great-grandfather, Rudolph Lederer, was Jewish," he answered. He explained there was a long line of Jewish ancestry in the Lederer and Koppl families, and sadly, many family members were incarcerated in Nazi concentration camps. That explained why several family members were buried in a Jewish cemetery.

All of this smacked like a startling revelation. And a saddening reveal: that I had had family members in concentration camps. But it brought me to a gradual realization—I might just be Jewish. Maybe that's why I could imitate Woody Allen and Mel Brooks so well. I mean, as a Christian, to be Jewish—that would be extraordinary. But I had to prove it somehow.

Testing the saliva told the story. The list of figures from my DNA test showed, at the top, 37.7 Ashkenazi Jewish. I felt like…like a man who discovers incredible wealth he didn't know about, buried in the backyard or stuffed away in a drawer. No—stuffed in his back pocket, and it's been riding around with him his whole life! Yet, better than any kind of monetary wealth, this was heritage. History. Being grafted into the original branch.

And so, wearing my first-ever kippah, which, in true Jewish style, boldly advertised the cemetery with address and phone number, I witnessed my first Jewish funeral.

We stood under tall, elderly trees, surrounded by old gravestones leaning this way and that, listening to the rabbi chanting in low, raspy tones. I bent near the marble headstone with golden letters glinting in the afternoon sun. Respectfully, Jeri and I shoveled a clump of dirt over Marketa's plot. Within my silence, mighty thoughts rolled like the ocean.

*Oh Lord, Mighty God, God of centuries, God of eternity, I thank you*
*for my family. I bless them. I thank you I am here. And I am Jewish.*

Christian eventually told me the story. My grandparents, Maria and
Rudolph, and their children, Gertrude (my mom Marguerite) and
Werner, were living in Ausick, Czechoslovakia, in 1938. In advance
of Hitler's arrival, they sent the children away to boarding schools,
Werner to Britain, Gertrude to France. After two years, they
returned to gather their children and moved to Canada. Then to
New York, and finally to California.

Neither Mutti nor my mom ever talked about these experiences. So
I never knew any of it until recently, and of course, they had both
passed away years ago. I learned that Mutti's father, my Opa
Lederer, was an eye doctor and was placed in a camp called There-
sienstadt. Aunt Marketa was there too, along with a dear friend of
the family, Henny Waas. Marketa and Henny were there as older
children and into adolescence.

This leads to part two of the story.

Before we made the journey to Teplice, Henny wrote to us. She
looked forward to all of us finally meeting, and had an idea.
"Teplice is not that far from Terezin," she explained, "which was the
camp where I was. If you want, we could walk through it. Or
maybe you don't want to. But I want to say good-bye to the old
place."

My first response? No. And how could she "say good-bye to the old
place"? How? When she lived in that "camp-ghetto" which served as
a transit camp for Czech Jews to be deported to concentration
camps and forced-labor camps in German-occupied Poland and

beyond? You would think she would never want to set foot in that place again.

Rather, it was as if she wanted to share this part of her life with us. It made me pause. I imagined it would be difficult. But, with Henny's buoyant attitude, it might be the experience of a lifetime. Though perhaps, like a journey "through the valley of the shadow of death." We had to think about it. And we made the right decision.

The city of Terezin, a little over five miles square, was built as a military fortress in the late 1700s. The square red-roofed buildings were arranged in a perfect grid, wrapped by a continuous wall around the edges of the city.

The four of us—me, Jeri, Henny and Henny's older daughter Jacky —walked along the cobblestone street into the city. People were scattered here and there. It was quiet. And lonely.

A few businesses and cafes lined the sidewalks, as well as museums, statues, and cars parked at the curbs. Even with the pervading stillness, Terezin held forth a distinctly European flavor. After walking through the morning, we sat at a street-side cafe, eating goulash.

Henny was calm, pleasant, very comforting. When she spoke, she sounded like Mutti. "Who would have thought," she mused, looking around, "that after so many years I could have a meal in Terezin, sitting down with friends. It's a good feeling."

During the walk, Henny told stories. I held a small recording device so I wouldn't miss a word.

At ten years old, Henny was hiding from the Nazis in a house in Holland. From her bed she was taken and loaded onto a train.

Without her parents, she went into the "cattle car" with seventy-two other people, and "nothing to eat, nothing to drink, and no toilet," she said. For three days.

Henny said she wouldn't tell us *all* the stories—some things she did not want to repeat. There was an elegance, a kindness, a clarity about this skinny little lady as she tour-guided us through a history that now belonged to me.

She first met Marketa in the camp hospital. The two girls became fast friends and stayed close to each other. Their rooms were in facing buildings. At night, they would lean out the windows and wave to each other.

Toward the end of our day, I asked Henny what it was like on the day she was freed. "We were on the street when the Russians arrived and the camp released us." A friend knew where her father was living, but he thought that Henny had died.

He was not at home when she arrived, now a young teenager, smoking a cigarette. Then she heard his steps in the stairwell.

"He came home, walked up the stairs, and then at once he saw me. He couldn't believe it. I had never seen him weeping like that, so upset, and so happy. He said later, it was the most beautiful moment of his life."

To be Jewish. It must mean to embrace a long history of deep sorrow and opposition. And yet, it means to be known as God's people, linked to Abraham, Isaac, and Jacob. If I can say it, to be fully Jewish is to embrace the long-prophesied Messiah and thereby be fully Christian. On the one hand, a troubling mixture, on the other, the best of both worlds.

*To dip your pen in the original ink,*
*To stain your fingers in a blood-red sink.*
*Grafted into the branch, the original link,*
*Changes everything you do and say and think.*

# Chapter 28

# LOSS BUT NOT LOST

One day, several years ago, my journey was divided into two halves.

On September 28, 2018, at age sixty-three, I had a heart attack.

I'd been trimming up the round bushes in our backyard.

"What's this feeling?" I asked me. It wasn't pain. Just a kind of slight pressure in my left arm. I'd felt it over the past few days, on and off, and now it had spread to my chest.

I didn't think it was anything. Until, on the couch, watching reruns on BritBox, we called Papa, Jeri's dad, and he instructed us to get it checked out—now.

At the clinic—I mean, why go to the emergency room for a "slight pressure"?—the attendant said I either did have, was having, or would soon have a heart attack.

So, an ambulance ride, a hospital stay, and two stents in my heart later, I was told what actually happened. The cardiologist flatly said, you had a massive heart attack.

Okay, well, *not* just a slight pressure.

The Lord graciously spared my life.

The three major arteries were seriously blocked. The cardiologist said most people who get to that point, well, you know. They don't live on earth anymore.

And so began a kind of second half of my (funny or sometimes not-so-funny) life journey.

Looking back, there was an unusual peace that accompanied me all the way through that event. A solid, deep, overarching, unshakable

PEACE inside, surrounding, and poured over every part of it. And of course, the blessing of having Jeri by my side.

I had several months of rehab, but thankfully, gradually, I got back to normal life, with the exception of a lingering tiredness.

My heart did have a percentage of damage, and I was dealing with sleep apnea, but I could resume my work remotely at Responsive Ed and, with a kind of new fervor, pursue the creative work I was called to do.

And during the recovery time, we were guided into a new church home.

We had been blessed to share fellowship with several churches across the past years, receiving and giving. From every church, deep friendships were established, even if our paths didn't cross as often, or maybe not at all.

There is something about Christian fellowship. Within that fellowship, friendships can bridge together in a short period and last a lifetime. Maybe John Fawcett said it best, in the hymn published in 1782, "Blest Be the Tie That Binds":

*Blest be the tie that binds*
*Our hearts in Christian love;*
*The fellowship of kindred minds*
*Is like to that above.*
*Before our Father's throne,*
*We pour our ardent prayers;*
*Our fears, our hopes, our aims are one,*
*Our comforts, and our cares.*
*We share our mutual woes,*

*Our mutual burdens bear;*
*And often for each other flows*
*The sympathizing tear.*
*When we asunder part,*
*It gives us inward pain;*
*But we shall still be joined in heart,*
*And hope to meet again.*

Speaking of meeting again, Mark and Bonnie had come to Arlington to visit us several times. One memorable time, their car pulled up our driveway, the door opened, and Mark, ever the comedian, rolled out onto the pavement, with "Geez! That was a long ride!"

Before my heart event, Jeri and I went to Colorado to see them and, of course all the Colorado Butlers which included Jen (and her boyfriend Espen), and Jaime, my two nieces.

Mark, in his early seventies, seemed a bit subdued, quieter than before, but otherwise his normal self. What I didn't know was that my brother's health was declining rapidly.

Some months later, in a text, I learned that he had kidney disease. I called, we talked, laughed, the usual humor suspects. But then another contact came from Jaime.

"Dad is in the final stages of kidney disease."

Bonnie called me shortly after that. She said Mark had had a fall and wasn't himself. She had found him standing in the bathroom, running warm sink water over his hands, in a daze. She surveyed the situation and, as a test, asked him, "Mark, what's my name?"

NOTE: You may remember that Mark was the master of ridiculous nicknames. So Bonnie was George, Skeeziks, Attila the Hun, Battle-Ax, etc.

He looked at her and said, "Bonnie." That was good, but not my typical brother.

Mark was declining. I was still in rehab therapy, but I wanted to go. I wanted to see him.

But these were the COVID-19 days. When he was hospitalized, even Bonnie was not allowed to be with him.

I told her I was coming. Bad idea. Already under pressure, she begged me not to come. She felt that if anything happened to me, she wouldn't be able to handle it. She ordered me to stay at home and get better. That's Bonnie. And I complied, of course.

I had a brief text volley with Mark. But he didn't make sense. He may have already been medicated, for this would be his last night on earth.

Bonnie and the girls were finally allowed to be with him. Knowing how much I wanted to be there, they sent a photo of themselves in his room. He was in bed with his face turned away from the camera. That was my last image, not easy to see, but I was so thankful to be, in some meager way, there with them. My family.

One more part I want to share with you. The phone call.

Bonnie, very upset. Sobbing, pushing out the words. "He's gone," and, "He went peacefully. He's not in pain anymore."

I slumped into a chair in my studio room. Jeri was in another chair near me. All the energy had gone out of me. It was like a big exhale and then, silence. Trying to process. Trying to think it through.

*How can he be gone? This is Mark. His name goes with Bonnie. I always say, "Mark and Bonnie." It's like salt and pepper. Peaches and cream. Crud steaks and super potatoes. How can I just say, "Bonnie"? That just doesn't work.*

The call was brief. Then over.

My time in the chair seemed like hours. My mother's passing, so many years ago, didn't have the impact of this passing. I had nothing to say and didn't know what to think. Life was a blank. A vacancy. Such a deep loss, even though I'd only seen him a handful of times across the last many years.

But something Bonnie said, it helped me out of my pit. "He's not in pain anymore." Okay. This was best *for Mark*. Maybe not for those around him, who love him. We have to get used to the loss. The gap that no other person in the world could fill. So yes, sorrow. But I wondered, *Am I just feeling sorry for myself? Grieving is normal, but should it give way to acceptance—even gratitude—at some point, maybe months or years down the road?*

For sure I knew, since Mark did not want a funeral, he didn't want people moping around about it. Bonnie and the girls got together and watched some of his favorite movies. That's, I know, what he would have wanted.

You may be reading this and relating to your own experience with a loved one. It's been said, that which is most personal is most universal. This happens to all of us, and finally, to each of us.

I began to think on the good times we shared. Of course, it was easy to remember those times since he was like a walking cartoon character. As I mentioned, from the Bugs Bunny cartoons, he was Da Boss, and I was Mugsy. That was funny because, in real life, just like the cartoon, he was shorter, and I was taller. But not faster.

By this I refer to the incredible speed at which he could recite the Catholic table grace. Breaking through the starting gate, praying in fast-motion words, and passing the finish line in about three seconds. And yet—and *yet*—clearly reciting all the words:

Bless us, O Lord, for these thy gifts we are about to receive from thy bounty through Christ Our Lord, amen.

He consistently prayed it. He consistently went to Mass with us when I was visiting them. And due to his time in Catholic school, I'm sure he was familiar with faith-life and acknowledged the Lordship of Christ, though he didn't attend church, that I know of, in his later years.

But he did show the love of Christ in how he took care of me and his family, their regular babies and fur babies. There was a nurturing love, along with the crazy nicknames.

So. Yes, Mark's passing was a loss. But I believe he wasn't, and isn't, lost. The much more appropriate word would be: Found.

> *The bench in sunlight at the dog-friendly park,*
> *The shiny green bench, the marker for Mark.*
> *Dogs were his pleasure, their every yip and bark,*
> *The "Dog Man of Monument," yup, that's Mark.*

# PART THREE
# Ever After

## Chapter 29

# NO PLACE LIKE HEAVEN

"Then close your eyes. Tap your heels together three times. And think to yourself, There's no place like home, there's no place like home..."[2]

Of course, these are perhaps the five most famous words in movie history.

"There's no place like home."

In *The Wizard of Oz*, produced in 1939, Dorothy, ready for home, clicks her ruby red heels together and repeats, "There's no place like home," and magically travels from the fantasy world of Oz to her home in Kansas.

You know the shoes Judy Garland wore in the movie? The ruby red slippers? They still exist.

I should know. I was there, gazing at them through protective glass.

We were visiting The Academy Museum of Motion Pictures in Los Angeles, just a few blocks from our daughter's place in LA. We walked into a large display room, dedicated to *The Wizard of Oz*, and there they were. The left shoe and the right shoe.

Sparkling beautifully. Very well preserved. Positioned against a spectacular background: A scene from the movie, enlarged to fill an entire wall.

The scene: The yellow brick road, surrounded by lush green grass and flowers.

On the road, we saw the Cowardly Lion, Dorothy, the Tin Man, and the Scarecrow, arm in arm, headed to Emerald City. The city's spires reached to the sky in gleaming magnificence. Though frozen in the image, the travelers were skipping along, singing, "We're off to see the Wizard, the wonderful Wizard of Oz!"

Life is certainly a journey.

In my little life, you've followed me from the principal's office to the upper bunk at ANA, from CHOC to TBN, from a *Zone* to a *Hut*, and from the streets of Terezin to the Yellow Brick Road. It's gone by in the blink of an eye.

And so it does, this journey from birth to death.

For the believer in Jesus, it's the journey from birth to death to life again.

Eternal life. Life in *heaven*.

And that's the part that seems difficult to grasp.

I understand birth. I'm all too familiar with death. But eternal life? Heaven above? Without being funny, Heaven seems out of reach. How can I relate to it?

And a bigger question: How can I long for it—with all my heart?

How can I—apart from being there in experience—be there in anticipation?

How can I be more *there* than *here*, feet on the ground, heart in heaven?

I want to live my days saying, "There's no place like heaven. There's no place like heaven..."

My concept of home has definitely changed across the years.

Home began as a house on Valley Vista. Then a dormitory. Then different houses in different locations.

But each physical structure felt less and less like true home. Being with people, family, church family, friends—that felt like home.

Then, after Mark's passing shook my life, a different kind of home shuffled to the top of all other homes. A place that was something else, somewhere else. A place beyond this planet. A heavenly home.

That concept really "hit home" a little less than a year ago.

I remember the night very clearly.

We were so tired...

We had sold the house. We'd lived there for nearly twenty years.

There was stuff crammed into every nook and cranny of that house, in drawers, closets and under the beds. We spent several months cleaning up and sizing down.

Finally, on that last day, after the moving van and the pickup truck with the trailer had gone, Jeri and I got into two cars, packed to the top with the final load of belongings, and left the house in Arlington.

We drove away, to build a new home in a new place.

I don't know why it makes me think of a song from the seventies, "Up, up and away, in my beautiful balloon!"[3]

And that makes me think of another up-up-and-away: Jesus and his final farewell.

Luke records it like this:

"And he led them out as far as Bethany, and lifting up his hands he blessed them. While he blessed them, he parted from them and was carried up into heaven. And they worshipped him and returned to Jerusalem with great joy, and were continually in the temple blessing God" (Luke 24:50–53).

I love this passage. Our Lord rises into the air, "carried up into heaven."

Okay. This is extremely good news about going to our new home, heaven.

Jesus knows the way.

It's up.

And, best of all, he is there.

That's my first guarantee for a happy home going.

So to help us look forward to heaven—really, really, *really* look forward to heaven—consider these **7 Heavenly Hints:**

## 1. JESUS IS ALREADY THERE.

**"...where I am you may be also." (John 14:3)**

Have you ever made a long trip to see someone you love? You knew the drive would be difficult. Twisting roads, foul weather, scary bridges. (I'm making this up.) But it would be worth it.

Because that's the way to your sweet grandmother's house. You love her home, her cooking, and how she plays the accordion. (Still making this up.) But the point is, the person is worth the perilous predicaments.

If Jesus is there—and he is—it's the most important place to be. The most hilariously happy place to be. The most serene, satisfying place to be.

Think of graduation day, a wedding day, or the arrival of a first child. All of these "threshold" experiences will be topped by the day we see Jesus. And embrace him and hear him say our name.

But if Jesus is already there, and has been for, I guess, from our perspective, a long time...What has he been doing? I don't mean to be trite. But I like the question because Jesus answered it before we asked it.

## 2. JESUS IS PREPARING A PLACE FOR YOU.

**"Let your hearts not be troubled. Believe in God; believe also in me. In my father's house are many rooms. If it were not so, would I have told you that I go to prepare a place for you? And if I go and prepare a place for you, I will come again and will take you to myself, that where I am you may be also." (John 14:1–3)**

Previous to this passage, Jesus told Peter that he could not follow him where he was going, but he could follow him later. Where he was going was to the crucifixion. But Peter must have been troubled, so Jesus gave him (and us) this beautiful, powerful reassurance: "I go to prepare a place for you."

I remember when my mom would make my bed. It was always just right. The pillow, the sheets, the covers—perfect. She prepared the bed for me. Can you imagine that Jesus—loving us enough to go to the cross for us—would prepare anything less than perfectly fitted for our benefit? Even for our pleasure, our endless delight?

Jesus did not want Peter, maybe his most difficult disciple, to be worried or troubled. He doesn't want the rest of us difficult disciples, worrisome wanderers, fearful followers, to question our future existence with him. Just because we can't see it, or even imagine it, doesn't mean it will be in any way unlikable.

Did you get a special cake for your birthday? I always wanted an ice cream cake, and most recently, an Oreo ice cream cake. That's my favorite, and I love taking the first cold, delicious bite. Mmmm. Okay, I'm getting off track here. But the point is: He is making a place just for *you*.

Repeat after me. Out loud. I'm serious. Please speak your part aloud.

ME: A place.
**YOU: A place.**
ME: Just for.
**YOU: Just for.**
ME: Me.
**YOU: Me.**

Let that sink in and cheer you up!

# 3. JESUS WILL PROVIDE A GLORIOUS DWELLING.

**"In my father's house are many rooms." (John 14:2)**

It's easy to forget that the Bible was written in languages other than English. And translated into many different translations and versions across the years. So when we read the word "rooms," there's a lot going on behind that one little word.

Rooms could be translated "houses" or "mansions." It can also be rendered "dwelling," or "abode," which leans more toward the idea of a family dwelling and a step beyond that even, conveying the idea of many people in the family of God, all abiding together.

This could spell delight or disaster, depending on your family background.

I grew up as a single child, raised by my mom and military schools. My wife grew up in a family of five. A dear family member of mine grew up in a family I thought was pleasant when I visited as a child, but in later years, I learned there was bitter animosity between her parents. She had a difficult family upbringing.

So when it comes to heaven, the idea of living together with others —a *lot* of others—probably raises different responses from different folks.

But this is a place *God* is making for us. The Creator. The Author. The Finisher. So you know it's going to be above and beyond our wildest, dearest, and highest expectations. God always goes above and beyond all we could ask or imagine (a reference to Ephesians 3:20).

Can you imagine dwelling in harmony, in endless joy? Living unin-terrupted in the presence of God? So it will be. One big happy family, bathed in the brightness of the Lord!

## 4. JESUS' PLACE WILL BE PLEASING TO EVERYONE.

**"And he who was seated on the throne said, 'Behold, I am making all things new.'" (Revelation 21:5)**

If heaven were designed by vote, we'd have a real problem.

Some would want a city, some a countryside, others a resort or an amusement park, or maybe an endless ocean with good fishing. None of these are bad ideas, of course. They're just exclusive to a certain group of people.

Some would want an everlasting concert of music (their particular style) with a never-ending banquet in the lobby of the concert hall. Yes, with dessert.

Okay, I guess I would want toys, and I know Mark would have insisted on dogs. The list of things and places would be...eternal!

Curiously enough, several kinds of dwelling places are mentioned in the Bible.

In the Book of Revelation, John reports seeing a heavenly city, prepared as a bride for her husband. He hears a loud voice announcing heaven as the place where God dwells with his people and describes God himself wiping every tear from their eyes. That's so personal—and powerful. Like a tender-hearted parent, wiping every single tear from their child's eyes.

In this astonishing place, there will be no more death, no pain, and on top of that, all things will be made *new*. All things. I would think that includes me and you!

John describes the Holy City, Jerusalem, with brilliant radiance, reflected in jewels and crystal (see Revelation 21). He says the streets are made of pure gold and the gates fashioned from pearl. So here you have a city, but there's more.

In the next chapter, John describes a river, bright as crystal, flowing through the city and on either side the Tree of Life, yielding fruit. Could this be a reference to the Garden of Eden? Could heaven be a tropical paradise? Could it be a restored Eden?

John says there will not be a temple. Wait—you mean, no churches, no synagogs? No tabernacles or buildings to meet in? What about Bibles and hymnals and, especially, potluck dinners with pie?

Well, again, Jesus makes everything better. God the Father has a higher plan, and the Holy Spirit comes to reveal it to us. We read (still in Revelation 21) that there *is* a temple. But it's not a temple like we would think. "...its temple is the Lord God the Almighty and the Lamb." Best. Temple. Ever.

Heaven will be a home everyone will love. Clouds or no clouds, harps or no harps, wings or no wings, it won't matter. God himself will be there. We will enter into his presence and there, have need of absolutely nothing.

# 5. JESUS WILL BE THE LIGHT OF HEAVEN.

**"And the city has no need of sun or moon to shine on it, for the glory of God gives it light, and its lamp is the Lamb." (Revelation 21:23)**

That verse leaves me speechless—at a loss for what words to type.

I may just leave this section blank, but then again, you're reading the book. So...

You think about the history of lighting fixtures. Well, maybe you don't, but stay with me here. There was firelight, torchlight, candlelight, oil-fed flames, gas-lit flames, electric light, lighthouses, searchlights, LED lights, and who knows what's next.

But what's really next is—the biggest, best, and brightest light ever experienced—Jesus Christ himself, along with God the Father, shining so brightly that all of the heavenly city is illuminated!

And whereas direct sunlight is dangerous to our eyes, this Son-light, more powerful than any other light, will be pleasing, perhaps even energizing or overflowing, flooding the very essence of our heavenly beings. Or so I imagine it.

I remember Chuck Smith talking about entering a darkened room. Let's say, a very dark room. You want to get rid of the darkness, but you don't know how. You try to force it out, blow it out, spray it out, swing around a broom or even a baseball bat—but nothing works. The only way to rid the room of darkness is to turn on the light.

We've all walked into a dark room and switched on or clapped on or instructed a voice response system to turn on the light. When it happens, it can be a shock—a totally dark room becomes totally bright. Takes our eyes a bit to adjust. Will heaven be like that?

Will we blink, standing in this place of pure, all-encompassing light? Because in heaven, I believe shadows do not exist.

Room light casts shadows. Sunlight casts shadows. Even a candle casts a shadow.

But I'm tired of shadows. Tired of evil, dark deeds. Unspeakable things shrouded in darkness, where sin reigns, and life intended for good is distorted, or damaged, or outright destroyed. I long for a shadowless life. Don't you?

Heaven will be different. Heaven's light will be everywhere. An unbroken, undimming, all glorious brightness. I want to be bathed in that glorious light. I want my family and dear ones to be captured by that glorious light. And I want the world to be transformed by God's loving, everlasting light in the meantime. I do. Don't you?

"This is the message we have heard from him and proclaim to you, that God is light, and in him is no darkness at all" (1 John 1:5).

John makes it very clear. No darkness. At all.

## 6. JESUS WILL TRANSFORM OUR BODIES.

**"...we shall be changed." (1 Corinthians 15:52)**

As heaven will be different from earth, heavenly people will be different than earthly people. I'm not sure exactly what that will look like, but I'm looking forward to it! I know it will be good beyond goodness and happy beyond happiness.

But I'm thinking, our heavenly bodies might be strangely familiar. As C.S. Lewis said:

"If we find ourselves with a desire that nothing in this world can satisfy, the most probable explanation is that we were made for another world."

Paul said this:

> "Behold! I tell you a mystery. We shall not all sleep, but we shall all be changed, in a moment, in the twinkling of an eye, at the last trumpet. For the trumpet shall sound, and the dead will be raised imperishable, and we shall be changed." (1 Corinthians 15:51–52)

It's funny to think of giving up sleep. I like sleep. And I like sleeping clothes. I like getting into pajamas, turning off the light, slipping under the covers, head on the pillow, and drifting off to sleepy-land. It's like entering a different world, isn't it? And then in the morning—or whenever—you wake up, entering the waking world again.

It's a change. Or an exchange. Let's say, a passage. So death for the Christian will be a passage, like going to sleep, but awakening to a very different place. And seeing a very special person. We will see our Lord.

"Beloved, we are God's children now, and what we will be has not yet appeared; but we know that when he appears we shall be like him, because we shall see him as he is. And everyone who thus hopes in him purifies himself as he is pure." (1 John 3:2–3)

This body I've got has served me well and continues to. But it's just an earth-house. And one day it will become a body fit for eternity. A heaven-house. That's going to happen. It's more real than earthly reality. It's what Lewis said. We were made for another world.

As believers, we *will* go there. We *will* be in heaven. We *will* be changed.

Oh, for this hope to resonate within in us! Oh, that I would let go of worldly preoccupations and set my mind on eternity. It doesn't mean I neglect my responsibilities. It means I embrace an eternal reality. But I still live here, in a temporary dwelling place. And one day my earth-house will be abandoned and my heaven-house occupied!

This is the kind of hope, the kind of expectancy I desire. I want a hope that pulses with every beat of my heart and flows through my soul like blood through my veins, coursing in and out of me like breath in my lungs.

With urgency, heart almost pounding, I want to "hope in Jesus." This kind of hope will purify me, John said. It will consecrate me. Change me. Isn't that so wonderfully mysterious?

I pray the temporary trappings of this world will be sifted out of me, will cease to preoccupy and control me. I want to live purely, unpolluted, impassioned for my Lord and breathing, longingly, for his eternal kingdom.

Maybe you and I can live like that. Walking softly, leaving deep, heavenly footprints.

Not just looking forward.

Looking up.

## 7. WE ARE WITH JESUS NOW AND FOR ETERNITY.

**"...with him in heavenly places..." (Ephesians 2:6)**

What I'm suggesting is this: eternal life can be something the Christian can experience *right now*. And now. And...wait for it...now. Every moment of every day. Or as close to that as is humanly possible. Honestly, I don't live that way. And maybe it's not possible. But I like a lofty goal, don't you?

Maybe I can put it this way. Believers stand in the doorway of eternity the moment they commit their lives to Christ: "Whoever believes in the Son has eternal life" (John 3:36). Eternal life is not only our future standing in Jesus but also our *current* standing in Jesus.

I have eternal life. It will change location, or rather, *I* will change location—when I die and enter his presence—but I live in the eternal majesty of his presence now. Twenty-four-seven as they say.

It still sounds confusing. Maybe it's like being granted citizenship in another country before actually moving there. The Bible says we are citizens of heaven, and this world is not our home. So in reality—spiritual reality—we are *here* but also in *eternity*.

Help me, Paul. Ephesians 2:4–6 reminds us, "God...made us alive together with Christ...and seated us with him in the heavenly places..." Past tense. Seated. It has already happened! Thank you, Paul.

The problem is, I forget where I really live and have to be reminded.

When Jeri and I made our journey to the Czech Republic and walked the streets of the city of Prague, we knew for certain we were in another country. A different language was spoken. Different foods were consumed. Signage and printing were unreadable to us.

If I may compare, respectfully, perhaps we should walk, drive, and live in this world with the feeling that this is not our home. Never to disdain other people or the human condition. Never to be above it but perhaps to be beyond it. To feel an "otherness" that gives us a distinction, a direction, and a dimension—namely, a God-given love for others, mingled with a heaven-sent perspective in which we live and breathe. Maybe it's a heavenly way of thinking, which glows over into a heavenly way of living.

As Paul said in Acts 17:28, "'In him we live and move and have our being.'"

Dear fellow believer, our Lord and Master is calling us to be people who have died to this world in order to live for Christ. We live *in* this world, but it doesn't mean we have to "dwell" here.

We live as people forgiven and transformed, yet we fall into earth-born or even sin-born patterns, often destructive. Even self-destructive and relationship destroying. We gravitate back and forth, pulled by earth, pulled by heaven. I believe there is a simple, one-word answer to these downfalls, and we've encountered it before. This word:

Dwell.

Or better:

Dwells.

"He who dwells in the shelter of the Most High will abide in the shadow of the Almighty" (Psalm 91:1).

We live here, but we don't have to dwell here.

Have you been walking on a hot, sunny day, and stepped into the shadow of a large, leafy tree? Being in the shadow of something implies being close to the something that casts the shadow.

Living a heavenly life, I think, involves dwelling, abiding, living, moving, and having our being in the shadow of Almighty God. The shadow that covers every day and reaches out across the world. Maybe that's the best definition of heaven on earth.

> *We pilgrims ever searching to find heaven on earth,*
> *We enter this certain bliss at the heart's second birth.*
> *We live in the shadow cast by heaven's sacred light,*
> *And we see both realities through heaven's holy sight.*

Chapter 30

# NO PLACE LIKE HOME

I'M WRITING THIS AS I FLY THROUGH THE CLOUDS.

Okay, I'm writing this as the airplane flies through the clouds. But I do too, because I'm sitting in a seat on the plane. And to my delight: it's a window seat!

Raising the shade lets in a splash of light, then reveals a spectacular skyline—with gigantic cloud sculptures, like mountains of cotton candy or soft-serve ice cream.

We soar through these clouds, with wisps of gauzy shapes passing by, flickering the light and the shadows.

My flight through the clouds takes me back to the description of Jesus' return to heaven: "While he blessed them, he parted from them and was carried up into heaven" (Luke 24:51).

And I wonder.

As Jesus was carried up, did he rise to the same altitude as this airplane? Not in this geographic location, I know, but was his body —just for a second—at the same height as this plane?

Probably, wouldn't you think? And did he rise into a billowy place like this, soaring among the clouds? And then, suddenly, did he pierce through dimensions, translating from our world to his eternity-world? Sorry for the strange questions. Probably comes from reading too many science fiction novels.

However, in Acts 1:9, Luke does give us a similar detail about our Lord's ascension:

"And when he (Jesus) had said these things, as they were looking on, he was lifted up, and a cloud took him out of their sight."

Just dreaming here, but could it be that right now, at this moment in earth-time, the plane and I are intersecting the vertical trajectory that believers will take, going to heaven to be with the Lord?

My Jewish self is saying, "Stop with the unanswerable questions already!"

"Sorry!" I answer, "but I'm on a roll!"

Looking through the little airplane window at the giant clouds—is it a sneak peek, a kind of teaser to what lies ahead, when we move from time to timelessness, from mortality to eternity? There it can truly, truly, *truly* be said, "There's no place like home."

May we be among those who, every day, in every way, are constantly finding HOME.

And if you've never found your personal relationship with Jesus, be sure to read the next chapter, an invitation to begin your Christian life both now and forever.

As John so beautifully said in Revelation 22:20, summing up the Book of Revelation, wrapping up the entire Bible, and voicing the cry of our hearts, "Come, Lord Jesus!"

*Amazing change, from place to Place,*
*Eternal change, when face to Face.*

Invitation

# HOW TO FIND HOME

Here's how to begin your delightful journey, your personal relationship with Jesus Christ. And how to secure yourself for heaven, your eternal home.

These are the Four Spiritual Laws from the tract by Dr. Bill Bright, founder of Campus Crusade for Christ.[4] Please read them carefully and be sure to pray the prayer at the end.

## THE FIRST SPIRITUAL LAW

**God loves you and has a wonderful plan for your life.**

"For God so loved the world, that he gave his only Son, that whoever believes in him should not perish but have eternal life" (John 3:16).

Jesus came that we may live life to the fullest. But what is blocking us from God's love? What is preventing us from having an abundant life?

## THE SECOND SPIRITUAL LAW

**Humanity is tainted by sin and is therefore separated from God. As a result, we cannot know God's wonderful plan for our lives.**

Romans 3:23 states, "for all have sinned and fall short of the glory of God."

Romans 6:23 adds, "the wages of sin is death." God created us to have fellowship with him. However, humanity brought sin into the world, and is therefore separated from God. What is the solution?

## THE THIRD SPIRITUAL LAW

**Jesus Christ is God's only provision for our sin. Through Jesus Christ, we can have our sins forgiven and restore a right relationship with God.**

Romans 5:8 shares, "but God shows his love for us in that while we were still sinners, Christ died for us."

First Corinthians 15:3–4 says, "For I delivered to you as of first importance what I also received: that Christ died for our sins in accordance with the Scriptures, that he was buried, that he was raised on the third day in accordance with the Scriptures."

Jesus taught that he is the only way to salvation: "I am the way, and the truth, and the life. No one comes to the Father except through me" (John 14:6).

## THE FOURTH SPIRITUAL LAW

**We must place our faith in Jesus Christ as Savior in order to receive the gift of salvation and know God's wonderful plan for our lives.**

In John 1:12 we read, "But to all who did receive him, who believed in his name, he gave the right to become children of God."

Acts 16:31 teaches, "Believe in the Lord Jesus, and you will be saved."

Salvation comes through grace alone, through faith alone, in Jesus Christ alone (Ephesians 2:8–9).

Are you willing to place your faith in Jesus Christ as your Savior and receive this free gift of eternal life? If so, do it now. There is no special prayer you must pray. Words will not save you. Only Jesus can save you. However, the following prayer is one you can use to tell God you are ready to accept Jesus Christ as your Savior:

> "Dear God, I realize I am a sinner separated from you. I can never reach heaven by my own good deeds. But you have made provision for my sin. Right now I place my faith in Jesus Christ as God's Son who died for my sins and rose from the dead to give me eternal life. Please forgive me of my sins and help me to live for you. Thank you for accepting me and giving me eternal life. In Jesus' name, Amen."

Note from Rod:

> If you've prayed that prayer, Jesus Christ is now Lord of your life. Congratulations! And welcome to the wonderful Christian life. The best journey a person can take. Be sure to get a Bible and find a church where you can meet other believers and grow in Christ.

> I'm glad to know we'll be in heaven together!

# END NOTES

1. Bill Bright, *Have You Heard of The Four Spiritual Laws?* (New Life Resources, 2005).
2. Victor Fleming, *The Wizard of Oz* (1939, Metro-Goldwyn-Meyer, Beverly Hills, California), film.
3. The 5th Dimension, vocalist. 1967. "Up, Up and Away." By Jimmy Webb. Recorded February 22, 1967.
4. Bill Bright, *Have You Heard of The Four Spiritual Laws*? (New Life Resources, 2005).

# ABOUT THE AUTHOR

**Rod Butler** grew up listening to the snapping of the typewriter as his father, John K. Butler wrote screenplays for Roy Rogers movies and TV shows such as *77 Sunset Strip* and *Death Valley Days.* Though John passed away when Rod was nine years old, the writing bug had bitten and Rod would go on to write, filling up books with poetry and stories, and eventually writing for television, print, online, and radio. Rod's radio career includes writing and hosting the nationally syndicated *Coconut Hut Radio Show* as Bongo Rod. He produced the animated series *Boy + Dog* for Daystar TV and Trinity Broadcasting Network (TBN), and has written hundreds of educational scripts for Responsive Ed. Rod is also a children's minister and a professional puppeteer. He is married with three grown children, who have also been bitten by the writing bug.

Read his blog at FilamentCity.com

 youtube.com/RodThePuppetGuy

# ALSO BY ROD BUTLER

More than 80 poems that will encourage, entertain, and be sure to bring a smile to readers of all ages. Order online at Amazon.com.

**A JUNIOR NOVEL PACKED WITH HUMOR & EXCITEMENT, CALLING KIDS TO BE BRIGHT LIGHTS IN THE WORLD.**

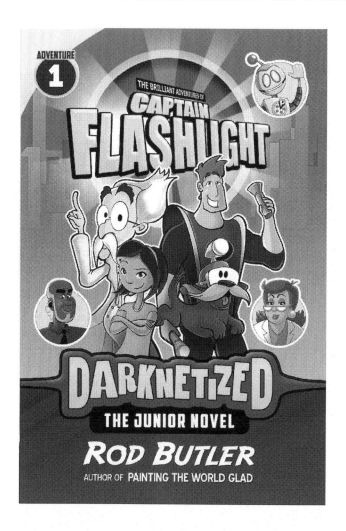

Filament City is covered in goopy purple darkness! Captain FlashLight, Neoni, and Blinkie discover that no matter how hopeless it looks, light will always conquer darkness! Junior Novel includes Reflection Questions. Order DARKNETIZED at Amazon.com.

Become a puppeteer and make your own puppets!

Check it out on youtube.com/RodthePuppetGuy

Made in the USA
Columbia, SC
08 June 2023

17710513R00159